My God Knows My Future

How God's Knowledge of the Future Protects My Freewill

Bishop Luis R. Scott
Columbus, GA

Dedication

This book is dedicated to my wife, Iris, who has shared her life with me for the past forty years. We have shared good times—and there have been many more of these—and the bad times—and there have been very few of these. God was gracious to me when He, in His infinite wisdom, made a way to bring Iris into my life. I am thankful to God for my life and grateful to Iris for her unconditional love. I am thankful for my four outstanding children and for the most awesome grandchildren anyone can imagine—Eliana, Addison, Ruly, David, Lincoln, Daniel, Esther, and Walker.

Bishop Luis R. Scott
Columbus, Georgia

Table of Contents

Foreword

I have spent the majority of my life peppering my father with questions about the deepest mysteries of God. This book is the product of many of those discussions over many years about the nature of God. In particular, this book is an answer to the questions that were raised after reading Dr. Boyd's book *The God of the Possible*. As I was searching the shelves of the many bookstores that I frequented, I came across a book that looked both interesting and provocative. What I found within the pages was not what I had expected. Rather than sharing insight, the book created confusion because it "felt" like the God that the book described was not the same God I had been taught to believe in and come to know.

Finding myself in this state of confusion, I took the questions about God's foreknowledge to my father. Dr. Boyd's book has served as the catalyst for many new and interesting discussions regarding the nature of God. As I have read this manuscript, I have been reminded of the times of conversation in living rooms and over kitchen tables as I grappled with my understanding of who God is.

I commend this book to you, the readers. One of the greatest benefits that I have found in this book is the examination of the underlying assumptions that the open theism position, as put forth by Dr. Boyd, uses to justify a revised understanding of God's foreknowledge. Some sections will require several reads to fully understand the problems in logic of open theism.

Prologue

While serving as a chaplain clinician at Eisenhower Army Medical Center in Fort Gordon, Georgia in 2001, I volunteered to serve my next assignment in South Korea. I had a well-designed plan. I would go to Korea for a year, and my wife, Iris, would stay at Fort Gordon so that my youngest son, Josué, could graduate from the same high school where he had started. After the Korea tour, I would return to Fort Gordon, give the Army three or four more years, and retire. Since we already owned a house in the area, this appeared to be the perfect plan. I was mentally, physically, and spiritually prepared to return to the Land of the Morning Calm. The orders for the assignment arrived in early January 2001 with a reporting date to Korea of July 18, 2001. The Army's plan and my plan were set, but God had other ideas.

In the first week of February 2001, while on call as the chaplain for the Eisenhower Army Medical Center, the hospital called me that Friday night, February 8, 2001, to visit with a patient who was suffering from cancer. The patient did not have much time to live. The patient's brother, Mr. Jackson (not his real name) and his wife had come from another state to spend the last few hours with her, and they wanted to talk with the chaplain on duty. The patient died the next day, Saturday,

February 9. I spent a few hours that Saturday with Mr. Jackson and his wife helping with the required hospital paperwork and providing spiritual support, the ministry of prayer, and encouragement.

The next day, before Mr. Jackson left the hospital, he stopped by the office to offer a word of thanks for my ministry to his family. Once we were in my office, he asked me a very strange question. He asked me about my future plans. I told him that I was reporting to Korea on July 18 and that after my overseas tour, I would stay in the Army a few more years and then retire. Mr. Jackson held my hand and said, "God sent me here to tell you that you are not going to Korea." Those words resonate with me to this day.

Needless to say, I was shocked by his words. I retained enough composure to tell him that the Army had already sent me the hard copy orders to report to Korea on July 18, 2001. Mr. Jackson responded with an emphatic, "So?" He added, "God sent me here to tell you that your mission here is not done." These last words were even more puzzling. While I did not doubt his sincerity, it was difficult to take his words at face value. What did he mean by saying that my mission was not done? What mission was that? What was God's plan for me?

Any person can make a prophetic claim, but this was a very specific statement that could be confirmed and verified within a few weeks. If the Korea assignment was deleted, then I would know that God had spoken. If the orders were not deleted, then God had not spoken. The Bible states that if a prophet claims that God has spoken, and the prophecy does not come through, then he is not a prophet (Deut. 18:22). All I could do was take a "wait and see" attitude.

As soon as I went home that morning, I told Iris about Mr. Jackson's words. She was as taken aback as I had been. We spoke about the possible implications and possibilities of what appeared to be a prophetic utterance. For the next few weeks, I tried to come up with one logical scenario that would stop my Korea assignment, but I could not come up with anything. How, exactly, would God do this? Iris and I were very nervous, but we decided to wait on God to see how he would get me out of the Korea assignment, if in fact Mr. Jackson spoke from God. The days and weeks passed by, and I continued with the preparations to go to Korea while praying that God's will be done.

On Thursday, April 20, 2001, just seven weeks before starting my transition vacation, I received a call from the Chief of Chaplains' office. I recognized the chaplain's voice on the phone. He asked me if I would like to attend the Command and General Staff College in residence. This is a prestigious senior military school, and at that time very few chaplains got selected for it each year. I answered that it would be a great blessing to attend the course after returning from Korea. The chaplain on the other end stated, "Good, then. You report to Fort Benning, Georgia, on January 6, 2002." I was incredulous about the date. I told the chaplain, "That reporting date puts me in Fort Benning only six months after reporting to Korea. Will you give me full credit for the overseas tour with six months of service?" He said, "Ah, don't worry about Korea. Your orders to Korea will be deleted Monday."

God wanted to let me know, specifically, that his plans for me did not include a trip to Korea in the year 2001. He wanted me to accomplish something for him or to experience something for my good. I tell you this story to illustrate the powerful blessing of depending on the God that knows what the future holds and chooses to make it known to us. Allow me to make several observations regarding Mr. Jackson's prophecy.

First, Mr. Jackson did not know me, and he could not have known that my name would be considered to attend the Command and General Staff College (CGSC) for two main reasons: (1) The selection board had met in November 2000, and I had not been selected. I had already attended a Defense Department School, CPE, and I was not eligible for a second military school. (2) My selection to CGSC came after the names of the chaplain chosen to attend the school had been released for more than four months. I was selected to replace a chaplain who must have dropped out of the school, possibly for medical reasons. Since I was selected as a last-minute substitute, no one could have known in February that, in April, a chaplain who had been selected to attend CGSC would be unable to attend the school.

Second, Mr. Jackson had no possible way to know when his sister was going to die. Additionally, he could not have known who the on-call chaplain at Eisenhower's would be for that week. He did not have access to the duty roster, and even if he had such access, I had never met him. The number of coincidences that would have had to be aligned in order for us to meet that weekend is staggering.

Third, Mr. Jackson could not have known in February that the Chief of Chaplains would need to select a substitute chaplain for the CGSC School in April. It was simply impossible for him to have known this information.

Fourth, the chaplain who called me did not know Mr. Jackson. He did not know that Mr. Jackson's sister was terminally ill at the hospital or that I was the duty chaplain for the first week in February. The chaplain from the chief's office could not have known about Mr. Jackson's sister, his trip to Fort Gordon, or our conversation. Therefore, the chaplain who called me could not have conspired with Mr. Jackson to change my assignment. He did not have that kind of authority anyway.

Finally, the Chief of Chaplains could not have considered Mr. Jackson's prophecy in their deliberation process because they did not even know that my chance encounter with Mr. Jackson had taken place two months earlier.

If God does not know the future, as open theists claim, the chain of events described above is some amazing guesswork. I cannot even conceive of the number of thoughts and actions that necessarily had to be coordinated in order to make my selection to Fort Benning, Georgia, possible. The open view of the future does not have a mechanism to explain the previous chain of events. These events took place exactly as I have described them.

Let's move forward two years. In March 2004, a civilian coworker asked me if I would be willing to conduct her daughter's wedding. She was getting married to a local doctor, and they had decided to hold the ceremony at the El Conquistador, a resort hotel in Puerto Rico. I agreed to conduct the wedding, the couple took the required premarital counseling meetings, and off to Puerto Rico we went. I arrived on the island on Friday, May 14, 2004. The rehearsal was that same Friday evening, and on that Saturday, John Dorchack and Angie Ramos were married. I returned home on Sunday, and as far as I was concerned, the entire process was over.

Dr. John Dorchak is a very specific kind of doctor—a spinal cord and back specialist. John's specialty includes disk replacement surgery, which was a fairly new procedure in the United States in 2004. I did not know when I conducted the wedding that, by January 2005, one of my lower back disks would completely collapse and make it virtually impossible for me to walk or stand for an extended period of time. As soon as I found out my condition, I petitioned the Army to approve John Dorchak as my doctor. Since John is a civilian doctor, the army had to give express permission for him be my physician. It approved him, and he diagnosed me with a severe case of disk degeneration. I needed to have disk replacement surgery. On May 19, 2005, I had the surgery with John as the attending physician.

The odds that (1) a Catholic family would search for a priest for months without finding one who could do their wedding, (2) that I would be asked by the bride's mother in an offhanded comment if I would be willing to do her daughter's wedding, (3) that the couple would accept my conditions for doing their wedding, (4) that the doctor's specialty was precisely what I would need a year from the wedding date, (5) that the Army would approve Dr. Dorchak as the surgeon despite the fact that he does not work for a hospital in the Army's list of approved surgeons, and (6) that the FDA would approve experimental disk replacement surgery in the United States in June 2004, two years after I arrived at Fort Benning, are simply staggering.

If I would have gone to Korea in July 2001, I would have never met Angie Ramos, the bride's mother. And she would have never asked me to conduct her daughter's wedding to the man qualified to perform the surgery I would need a full year after the wedding.

Someone may say that all of these events are just weird coincidences. My response to that is that as far as I was concerned, in May 2004, I was doing a favor to a friend by conducting her daughter's wedding. However, from God's perspective, God was arranging a meeting between my surgeon and me. Only a God with foreknowledge can arrange the chain of events that started on February 10, 2001, when a stranger predicted that I would not go to Korea. The chain of events unleashed by Mr. Jackson's prophecy concluded when John Dorchak performed my lower back disk replacement surgery on May 19, 2005.

These events represent four years of anticipation in which thousands of uncreated and unrelated events came together to accomplish God's purpose. This experience is not evidence that I am more deserving than any other child of God. I assure you that I am not. God deals with each one of us equitably, even if not equally. Only the God of foreknowledge could have foreknown and made known the series of events that led to the fulfillment of Mr. Jackson's prophecy. My personal example is not the ultimate proof of God's foreknowledge, but it goes a long way to illustrate that, indeed, all events belong to God.

There are things that we know. There are things we do not know. And there are things that we do not know we don't know.
—Donald Rumsfeld

Introduction

Samuel Rutherford was quoted as saying,

Duties are ours, events are God's; When our faith goes to meddle with events, and to hold account upon God's Providence, and begins to say, "How will You [God] do this or that?" we lose ground; we have nothing to do there; it is our part to let the Almighty exercise His own office, and steer His own helm; there is nothing left for us, but to see how we may be approved of Him, and how we roll the weight of our weak souls upon Him who is God omnipotent, and when we thus essay miscarries, it shall be neither our sin nor our cross.[1]

The Title of the Book

My God Knows My Future is a book that addresses the perceived contradiction between God's foreknowledge and moral freedom. Open theists have resisted the deterministic motif, justifiably so, but in order to reconcile the perceived contradiction between foreknowledge and

---

[1] Samuel Rutherford, quoted in Ruth Bell Graham, *Prodigals and Those Who Love Them* (Colorado Springs, CO: Focus on the Family Publishing, 1991), 106.

freewill, they determined that moral freedom (freewill) was a more clearly defined concept, and a result they rejected foreknowledge. This book will address the issue of foreknowledge as the divine attribute that guarantees moral freedom.

My God Knows My Future proposes that God safeguards human freewill through the natural restraint he imposes on his power and knowledge. That is, God could impose his will over us because the has the power and knowledge to do so. The prophet stated that "For I the Lord do not change; therefore you, O children of Jacob, are not consumed" (Mal. 3:6). God's unchanging character is the reason Israel continued standing. God's faithfulness to his covenant with Abraham served as a restraining promise to his anger. God's love, mercy, compassion, and faithfulness that restraint his power and knowledge.

The humongous error of theological determinism is their blindness to God's impartiality, which is never addressed by anyone within classical theology. Open theists know, instinctively, that human beings are morally responsible and accountable to God for their choices and actions. Therefore, it is not possible for God to preordain every thought, choice, and action while demanding moral responsibility. Since theological determinism has defined foreknowledge as being determinative, open theists believe they have no choice but to redefine foreknowledge and reject it. They have reasonably concluded that if determinism is true, then, it is impossible for God to demand moral accountability from morally predetermined individuals. I will wrestle with these issues and provide what I believe is a more biblical and reasonable option.

The Bible is the written record of God's revelation of his character, essence, and nature. We have enough information about God to engage him in a personal and intimate relationship. In spite of the knowledge we can claim about God, our God is couched in mystery. We cannot fully grasp this God, nor can we explain him. This has been a source of frustration for theologians throughout the centuries. Many have simply given up on the endeavor and have concluded that faith is irrational and that we just need to accept God for what the text says without the need to inquire any further. Others have tried to explain God to the point of reducing him to a simplistic human understanding.

Open theism falls in the camp of those who attempt to define God from a human point of view to satisfy the desire of a philosophical reconciliation between God's sovereignty and human freewill. Open theism's attempt to redefine God's knowledge fails mostly because they do not provide an affirmative alternative to God's knowledge. They get God all wrong because their reaction to theological determinism assumes that either determinism is correct, or that they are correct. By using the erroneous presuppositions presented by theological determinism, open theists have reached the wrong conclusions regarding God's cognitive attribute of foreknowledge. Their conclusions are based on the false premise that theological determinism is necessary to understand God's sovereignty.

Purpose of This Book

The purpose of this book is to present a theological, philosophical, and hermeneutical challenge to the theological system known as the "open view of the future" or "open theism." Proponents of open theism include Clark Pinnock, John Sanders, David Basinger, William Hasker, and Gregory Boyd, among others. The most significant claim open theists make is that God does not know the future.

I will make reference to some of open theism's proponents, but the focus of our attention will be on Gregory Boyd's book *The God of the Possible*. Boyd's book was written to reach the layperson in the church. As such, it is more dangerous than the others. Boyd's basic premise, which is shared by the others, states that God does not know the future because the future does not exist, and "there is *nothing definite there for God to know!*"[2] The logical conclusion to open theism suggests that if God knows the future, then God is the author of evil or must find redeeming value in evil, and God's foreknowledge nullifies humanity's freewill. I believe open theists are wrong on both points.

First, very few people dispute that evil exists in this world. However, it is important to note at the beginning of this discussion that evil is not a creation or a thing per se. Evil is the unnatural result of the

---

[2] Gregory Boyd, *The God of the Possible* (Grand Rapids, MI: Baker Book House, 2001), 16.

human decision to reject God's goodness. As such, evil, in its broadest definition, is the absence of good and not an actively created *thing* in itself. Therefore, God can never be justly blamed for evil's presence in general or for human sin in particular. Evil is an internal distortion—a virus if you will—that emerged from within the system and not the result of God's creation, even though God foresaw its appearance. Thus, God had to eradicate evil from within the system, and he achieved that very goal with Jesus's entrance into the world, his death on the cross and his resurrection.

Second, freewill is God's creation in that he gave human beings the innate ability to distinguish between good and evil. This ability includes the option to love or reject God without external compulsion. Both the ability to distinguish good from evil and the freedom to accept or reject God occur within the created order. This means that God's essence and personhood are not harmed, changed, or distorted by human behavior. God exists outside his creation, but human behavior is confined to the close biological system we call the earth.

Libertarian freewill has been defined as giving people absolute freedom to the point of even influencing God's thinking. If we understand that God and people exist in two distinct and separate realms, we have to conclude that this is a false assertion. Human decisions are confined to the created order and cannot extend to God's realm. That God exists outside the created order is not a debatable point. Solomon, referring to God's dwelling place, stated, "But will God indeed dwell on the earth? Behold, heaven and the highest heaven cannot contain you; how much less this house that I have built!" (1 Kgs. 8:27). Clearly, any human violation of God's commandments has dire consequences for people, but humans do not have the power to reach to heaven and influence God in any way.

People have used freewill to make immoral choices. These choices are not an indictment on God's character, even though he gave people the ability to make those choices. People's abuse of freewill is the external expression of a diseased heart. This disease is a systemic malady that arose from within the human heart (Jam. 1:13–14). In other words, the sin that rejects God was born from within the system (Rom. 5:12). People are, therefore, able to exercise freewill independently of God's compulsion, but not outside of God's created order. God continues to oversee his creation without the need to violate human freedom or the need for constant intervention.

There are three main reasons that human freedom will always remain under God's sovereignty: (1) freewill is confined to the created order, (2) human freedom has the inherent limitation imposed on it by God's design of the human body and psyche, and (3) freewill remains subservient to God's sovereignty because its exercise remains trapped within God's creation.

Any discussion regarding humanity's knowledge of the future is inevitably crippled by the intrinsic human limitation that confines their life experiences to the temporal. That is, our thinking about the future is restricted to abstract concepts that are not connected to any historical or experiential knowledge of the future. People can never experience the future. Humanity marches toward the future in incremental little steps in a persistent present tense. God, on the other hand, exists independent and outside of time. Any definition of the future cannot equate the human perception of it with God's. God exists in an eternal present tense in which human time is a by-product of his creative activity. We, then, cannot define God's view of time from the creature's perspective. Our cognitive ability is limited by our temporal existence, and knowledge of the eternal is confined to what God chooses to reveal to us.

We will explore several critical areas of study regarding God's involvement in human affairs: God's foreknowledge and its relationship to human freewill, God's foreknowledge and its relationship to prophecy, and God's foreknowledge as a noncausative divine attribute. Additionally, we will review the hermeneutics of open theism, attempting to show that they are incredibly naïve or intentionally deceptive.

Finally, we will demonstrate how prophecy becomes the open view's Achilles' heel. Open theists cannot escape God's attribute of foreknowledge, especially as it relates to prophetic revelation. All of the platitudes offered by open view theologians regarding freewill, evil in the world, or the practicality of their basic premises, pass or fail at the altar of the prophetic word. Until, and unless, open view theologians get past the prophecy roadblock, their entire system is demonstrably a poorly constructed house of cards.

We will address the question of God's motivation to engage humanity with his salvation plan. We cannot determine God's ultimate motivation to become involved with humans. However, biblical revelation opens a window to God's motives. Allow me to share three possible ways God engages people to unfold the salvation plan.

First, God acts exclusively according to his character. It is essential to understand that God does not violate his Word. For instance, God's character can be described as both just and good. His justice demands punishment for sin. His goodness demands that grace be extended to the sinner in the form of forgiveness (Ps. 130:3–4). In order for God to remain faithful to his character, he decided to take upon himself the penalty for sin to satisfy his justice. In doing so, he became free to extend his grace to the world. Paul writes that "in the gospel (good news) the justice of God is revealed" (Rom. 1:17). God demonstrated his goodness when he sent Jesus to be our substitute, and he revealed his justice when Jesus paid the penalty of sin through his death. God is free to forgive people's sins because Jesus paid the sinners debt in full.

Second, God established the salvation plan according to his goodness. Outside of God's love, there is nothing in biblical revelation that requires God to take a proactive approach to human behavior. From the moment that Adam and Eve rejected God's grace to the cross of Jesus, God led history through the maze of human affairs to bring salvation to all who believe.

Third, God responds when people come to him in faith. Faith is the element that connects us to the eternal, and yet, people experience faith in the present. Human faith, a present reality for humanity, is the reason God is totally and unchangeably committed to dealing with us in the present. God never denies us a blessing today based on his knowledge of future sins. Since we do not know how we are going to behave tomorrow, it would be unjust for God to withhold a blessing in the present day based on decisions only God knows we will make tomorrow.

This is a critical principle. God's faithfulness is shown in that he remains faithful even if we are unfaithful (2 Tim. 2:13). God responds to our faithfulness today without considering our possible unfaithfulness tomorrow. God will worry about our unfaithfulness tomorrow when tomorrow comes. Even Jesus made this statement about our worries. He said, "Therefore do not worry about tomorrow, for tomorrow will worry about itself. Each day has enough trouble of its own" (Matt. 6:34). Jesus was encouraging us to live for him today because God will take care of us tomorrow. The God of open theism cannot make such a promise.

In the following chapters, we will discuss some misconceptions about God's character contained within open theism's theology. Open theists do not know, or have decided to ignore, that God is committed to deal with us in the present time. We are irrevocably tied to the present, and God meets us there. This commitment is an intrinsic aspect of God's character. He declared that he is the eternal "I Am that I Am" (Ex. 3:14).

Open theism cannot, and should not, survive as a theological system until its proponents have adequately answered questions in the four following areas: First, they must provide a clear definition of prophecy within their system. We are looking for precise definitions of terms and how the God of the open view can predict anything related to people if he cannot know any future and uncreated human activity.

Second, they must answer how the God of open theism answers prayers that have unintended consequences to him. Again, we need precise definitions of terms that go beyond the platitudes of saying that open theism is more practical than classical theology. They need to explain how God answers prayers without knowing the ultimate consequences those answers would have on the people who received them.

Third, they have to explain how God's perfect knowledge of the present does not infringe on humanity's libertarian freewill in the present. They argue that if God has foreknowledge, by necessity, that knowledge will eliminate freewill. If the principle is true about the future, it must also be true about the present. Their missing piece is that information, both, present and future is not inherently causative. Open theists, like classical theologians, do not even address the issue of non-causal information.

Finally, they must also explain how information possessed by a free agent becomes causative for the behavior of another free agent. They must be able to make a credible argument that demonstrates a direct cause-and-effect correlation between information and causality.

Failure in any one of these categories destroys the basic premises of open theism—that is, that God cannot know the future because it does not exist to be known. Failure to address these four issues exposes open theism for what it is—nothing more than a postmodern rehashing of Lorenzo McCabe's discredited nescient doctrine and a knee jerk reaction to theological determinism.

Trust in the LORD with all your heart and lean not on your own understanding; in all your ways acknowledge him, and he will make your paths straight.

—Proverbs 3:5–6

Chapter ONE
Definitions of Terms

This book is a critique of the theological perspective called the open view of God, open view of the future, or open theism. These terms are used interchangeably, and they mean that the future is as unknowable to God in the same way that it is unknowable to people. In other words, God experiences the future like humans—in a linear, sequential manner—being absolutely confined to a present tense existence. Open theism's fundamental claim is that the future does not exist and, as such, not even God can know anything about it. I believe this theological perspective is an attempt to bring balance to the deterministic view, which is a distortion of God's character. Since open view theologians are trying to define their terms using the same theological framework of theological determinism they come to the wrong conclusions based on the wrong premise. That is, they claim that God cannot know the future because determinism is incompatible with moral freedom, and they are correct on this point.

However, I believe they err in fighting theological determinists on their terms instead of presenting a different approach. That is, open theists should have presented the evidence that theological determinism is incompatible with biblical theology, but instead they chose to attack God's attribute of foreknowledge. Determinism is a theological error, but not because it believes in foreknowledge. Determinists are wrong because it erroneously, in my view, assumes that foreknowledge is causative, which is not, as we will demonstrate in this book.

Open view theologians claim that God does not know the future, but not because God's knowledge is limited. They support the idea that God knows everything that exists. However, since the future does not exist, and it is not there to be known, then, it follows that God cannot know it. They suggest that since God knows that the future does not exist, it is not a challenge to God's omniscience to say that God does not know the future. This argument gives the appearance of congruency and logic, but I can identify at least one problem with open theists' logic. For instance, they teach that there is no biblical or historical support in church history for foreknowledge, even though the word itself is used at least twice in the Bible (Acts 2:23; 1 Pet. 1:2) in reference to events God knew in advance, and contrary to thousands of prophecies are based on foreknowledge. The basic tenet of open theism has as its ultimate goal the redefinition of God's attribute of omniscience and not the so-called nature of the future.

The survival of open view theology hinges on how effectively its proponents can establish hermeneutical principles that explain away God's omniscience and biblical prophecy. Both classical orthodoxy and open theism claim to use a literal interpretation method, which has served the church well for centuries. However, open theists arrive at opposite conclusions that end up changing the historical definitions of *omniscience* and *foreknowledge*. For example, open theism has redefined God's omniscience so that it no longer means that God has exhaustive knowledge of the past, present, and future. Within open view theology, God's attribute of omniscience means that God knows all there is to know, with the exclusion of any information about the future because the future is not there to be known. Even though this book is not specifically about hermeneutics, it is impossible to debate open theism without addressing its hermeneutics.

A Description of Open Theism

Open theism kicked off as an organized theological system in 1994 with the book, *The Openness of God: A Biblical Challenge to the Traditional Understanding of God*.[3] In it, Pinnock, Rice, Sanders, Hasker, and Basinger wrote what has been the most comprehensive exposition of the openness view. Additionally, Gregory Boyd, pastor of a large church in Minnesota and former professor of theology at Bethel University in St. Paul, has written extensively regarding this subject utilizing less theological language to reach church laity. Boyd's book *The God of the Possible* was written, according to the author, to simplify the openness view to the average church member.[4]

Boyd embraced the concepts being propagated by open theism that can be traced to the 1800s Methodist preacher and philosopher Lorenzo Dow McCabe, even if open theists do not acknowledge the connection.[5] McCabe had advocated what has been described as the "nescient" [literally, "not knowing"] theory of God.[6] McCabe argued that human freewill necessitates that God cannot know future human events in order for freewill to remain truly free. He suggested that God, as a matter of necessity—and inherent in his act of creation of humans with freewill—submitted himself to human activity as a precondition to his knowledge.

McCabe also argued that "absolute divine prescience [literally, "absolute knowledge"] is contradicted by biblical writers."[7] This was a novel approach to theology, and it never received a wider consideration until the emergence of the openness doctrine in the 1980s. I find it curious that McCabe could find God's foreknowledge (*prescience*) to be contradictory to biblical teaching, while at the same time finding that the *nescient principle* (a principle that has never been supported in church history) was perfectly congruent with biblical doctrine. McCabe's conclusion appeared to interpret biblical revelation as the

---

[3] Clark Pinnock, et al., *The Openness of God: A Biblical Challenge to the Traditional Understanding of God* (Downers Grove, IL: InterVarsity Press, 1994).
[4] Gregory Boyd, *The God of the Possible.*
[5] Ibid, 115.
[6] George M. Porter, http://www.opentheism.info/index.php/pages/george-m-porter/, 2007 (Accessed November 2010).
[7] Ibid.

exact opposite of its normal reading and meaning. To my knowledge, there is no direct or indirect evidence in Scripture that supports a nescient doctrine of God. McCabe's nescient necessity of God was intended to uphold the "libertarian freedom" of humanity, which has become a basic tenet of open theism.[8]

Boyd began his journey into the openness doctrine as a viable theological alternative as early as 1984. In his book *Letters from a Skeptic,*[9] Boyd discussed several letters exchanges with his father during the 1980s. One such letter answered his father's question regarding God's omniscience. Boyd answered as follows:

> Your question in your last letter about God's foreknowledge is a good one, but I think it's based on a misconception of what God's omniscience (His knowing everything) entails. In the Christian view God knows all of reality—everything there is to know. But to assume He knows ahead of time how every person is going to freely act assumes that each person's free activity is already there to know—even before he freely does it![10]

Boyd made three misleading suggestions, and one cleverly disguised *bait-and-switch* statement, in this quote. First, he described the concept that God knows everything as a "misconception." It was obvious that his father's understanding of omniscience must have come from his reading of classical theology. Boyd's suggestion that his father had misunderstood the orthodox definition of *omniscience* was not accurate. His father had asked the question based on the traditional interpretation of omniscience, but Boyd created the impression of a misconception to advance his new understanding of omniscience.

Second, Boyd erroneously suggested that his limited definition of "God's knowledge of all reality" is the traditional Christian view of omniscience. It is not. While on the surface this appears to be a sensible statement, the fact is that he defined "all of reality" very narrowly to exclude any information God may have of any future human activity. He purposely placed the future outside of knowable reality to confuse

---

[8] John Sanders, "Welcome to the Open Theism Information Site," http://www.opentheism.info, 1996 (Accessed July 2012).
[9] Gregory Boyd, *Letter from a Skeptic: A Son Wrestles with His Father's Questions About Christianity* (Grand Rapids, MI: Baker Book House, 2000).
[10] Boyd, Letter dated 17 April 1989, 29.

his readers. I believe this is a major problem for Boyd and other open view theologians. As we shall see later, he also stated, contradicting himself, that God has a remarkable ability to know specific future events.

Third, Boyd suggested that God's knowledge is intrinsically contingent upon human behavior, agreeing with McCabe. His contention was that since future human actions have not yet taken place, they are unknowable because they are not "there to [be] known." This statement could be true only if he was making reference to historical and concrete facts. However, we need to take into account that information exists in a realm completely independent from concrete events. To suggest that the Christian view of omniscience has ever included a nescient principle of God is misleading and factually erroneous.

Then, Boyd gave us the bait-and-switch: "But to assume he knows ahead of time how every person is going to freely act assumes that each person's free activity is already there to know." This statement is astounding. Contained in the statement is the assumption that freely chosen decisions cannot be known in advance because they are not concrete acts. That is, future decisions are not "there to know." It is important to note that something does not have *to be there* to be known. I am not arguing that future events exist to be known as historical realities. My argument here is that God knows the future in the form of noncausative information. The Bible instruct us that God is unique and different from idols in that he, and he alone, knows the future in the form of exhaustive, noncausative information. Otherwise, God would not be any different than a mute idol made of a dead tree. This is the reason that God can "make the future known" while idols cannot (Is. 46:10).

In his summary of open view theology, William Hasker wrote that "God has, in his sovereign freedom, decided to make some of his actions contingent upon our requests and actions."[11] This is an extraordinarily broad statement with grave implications for God's

---

[11] William Hasker, "The Incompatibility of Libertarian Free Will and Divine Timelessness." http://www.opentheism.info/index.php/william-hasker/the-incompatibility-of-libertarian-free-will-and-divine-timelessness/, April 1996 (Accessed July 2012).

character. Hasker's assertion might be true only if it was a reference to the human experience of answered prayers. God answers prayer in response to our faith. However, we do not have any specific information regarding God's *process* to answer our prayers. Hasker's extrapolation that God's response to faithful prayers is an indication of his ignorance of the future is unwarranted, or that answering prayers make God subjective to human wishes. Actually, trusting God's answers to prayers would be very dangerous if he did not know the future unintended consequences of his own answers. To suggest that human freewill necessitates God's ignorance of future human events is not logical. Human freewill is a natural function within God's created order, and nothing people do with their freewill within the confines of our closed biological system could influence or contradict God's knowledge.

Open theologians have borrowed from Greek philosopher Alexander of Aphrodisias, who "defended a view of moral responsibility we would call *libertarianism* today."[12] Greek philosophy had no precise term for *freewill,* so their discussion was "in terms of responsibility, or about what "depends on us."[13] He argued that some events do not have predetermined causes. In particular, people are responsible for self-caused decisions and can choose to do or not do something. Alexander of Aphrodisias denied the foreknowledge of events that was part of the Stoic identification of God and nature. His problem, as it related to God, was that he understood foreknowledge from a deterministic as opposed to a noncausal information motif.

Open theists have latched onto the libertarian freewill concept by using the same concepts proposed by Alexander of Aphrodisias. Cicero later stated that "if there is freewill, all things do not happen according to fate; if all things do not happen according to fate, there is not a certain order of causes; and if there is not a certain order of causes, neither is there a certain order of things foreknown by God."[14] Again, Cicero worked from the assumption that foreknowledge necessitates a deterministic understanding of reality, which it does not.

---

[12] Alexander of Aphrodisiac. http://www.informationphilosopher.com/solutions/philosophers/alexander/ (Accessed March 2013)

[13] Hasker, http://www.informationphilosopher.com/freedom/ libertarianism.html, 3.

[14] Ibid, 4.

Open theists offer two reasons in support of libertarian freewill. First, according to Pinnock, "the Bible itself assumes libertarian freedom when it posits personal give and take relationships."[15] This concept could be directly credited to Alexander of Aphrodisias and Cicero, as noted in the previous paragraph. It appears that open view theologians have accepted the definitions offered by Greek philosophy regarding freewill. Open theism argues that libertarian freewill is the essential element for the reciprocity between God and humans. However, in order for this reciprocity to be a truly free exchange between God and humanity, they say, God has to abandon his eternal place to accommodate humanity's freewill. While I agree with the basic tenets of freewill, I believe the biblical model is moral freedom. The difference between these two concepts has to do with their scope. Libertarian freewill is defined as a freedom without restrictions, while moral freedom is limited to moral choices. The most obvious example is of this principle is the Garden of Eden story. Adam and Eve were free to roam the Garden, but God held them responsible for their moral choices only. The same remains true today.

Kenneth M. Gardoski provided a helpful summary of the four pillars of open theism, and he added a fifth one. John Sanders has stated, and Clark Pinnock concurs, that there are four major points in the open theistic model: (1) the love of God; (2) the conditionality of God; (3) the general providence of God; and (4) the libertarian freedom of humanity. Gardoski added a fifth pillar, which actually could be considered the first: (5) the reciprocity of God. The reciprocity principle in the God-world relationship plays a critical role in Pinnock's early stages of his pilgrimage. Similarly, Sanders summarized the main points of open theism with an emphasis on what he called "relational theism."[16]

Later Boyd provided a theological defense of open theism in layman's language with his book *The God of the Possible*.[17] Some call this perspective "the open view of God," but Boyd prefers the phrase "the open view of the future."[18] Boyd's fundamental premise, which

---

[15] Clark Pinnock, *Most Moved Mover: A Theology of God's Openness* (Grand Rapids and Carlisle: Baker and Poternoster, 2001), 115.

[16] Kenneth M. Gardosky, "Open Theism." *Baptist Bible Seminary* (Clarks Summit, Pa., Year).

[17] Boyd, *The God of the Possible*.

[18] Ibid, 15.

affirms Pinnock and Sanders, is that the future does not exist and is not available for God to know.[19] This is a crucial declaration in open view theology, and we need to keep it in mind as we evaluate this theological perspective.

If God does not have access to the future, then prophecy—which is a central aspect of God's revelation of his character—must not be part of the biblical record. However, biblical evidence indicates that Jesus fulfilled more than three hundred prophecies. The argument can be made that he self-fulfilled the prophecies because he knew them. However, we know of prophecies that Jesus could not personally control even if he had known them. For example, while Jesus was hanging on the cross, the soldiers cast lots for his garments and divided his clothes among them. This human event was predicted by David when he said, "They divide my garments among them and cast lots for my clothing" (Ps. 22:18).

The reader needs to keep in mind that David made this prophecy more than eight hundred years before the crucifixion. What are the odds that David could have accurately predicted that a group of soldiers would be casting lots for Jesus's clothing at the foot of the cross? Only the God of foreknowledge could have made such an astounding prediction. The God of the open view cannot even predict what will happen tomorrow, much less an event that was 800 years removed to be carried out by pagan soldiers at the feet of Jesus's cross. The openness God could not have predicted this event, period. This was a distinctively human event that did not exist at the time that David wrote Psalm 22. In spite of this, open theists have assured us that future human events cannot be known. Later in his book, Boyd attempted to diminish the damage done by the fundamental premise that rejects knowledge of the future with the creation of the concept he called the "partly settled future."[20]

I will refer back to these two statements often as a reminder of the inconsistencies within openness theology. The first statement that the future does not exist and cannot be known creates the false impression that divine and human realities are identical. Additionally,

---

[19] Boyd, 16–17.
[20] Ibid, 54.

he erroneously assumes that knowledge is limited to concrete events, which it does not. Clearly enough, people do not exist in the future, and it is impossible for them to have experiential knowledge of the future. People experience events in a fixed linear timetable. This is a self-evident reality for the human experience. The question that concerns us is whether God has the same limitations regarding time as people do.

Purpose for *The God of the Possible*

Boyd's main purpose was to provide the theological and philosophical rationale for the open view of the future. He stated his intentions this way:

> The careful reader may have already discerned a subtle but very important point regarding this debate about God's foreknowledge—namely, it is not really about God's knowledge at all. It is rather a debate about the nature of the future.[21]

While Boyd's declared intent was to discuss the "nature of the future," I do not believe he achieved his purpose. The careful reader will notice that the opposite is true. Boyd's book *is not* about the nature of the future but about the nature of God's knowledge. His statement was an attempt to convince the readers that God's attribute of omniscience was not in question. However, the only substantive statement that Boyd makes about the nature of the future in his book is that the future does not exist.[22] Then, he spent the rest of the book giving the reasons that God cannot know the future. The discussion was about God's knowledge and not about the nature of the future. Boyd wants the readers to reach a specific conclusion that flows from his logic—if the future does not even exist in the form of noncausative information, then no one (including God) can know it.

Whatever the future is, open theists have concluded that it is a definable reality that resides outside of God's scope of knowledge. Nevertheless, even though open theists have argued that the future does not exist, they assure us they know enough of the future to be able to define its very nature. We need to make a clarification here. Since the

---

[21] Boyd, 15.
[22] Ibid, 16.

future does not exist within open theism, then it seems unreasonable for open theists to define its nature with any degree of certainty. I suggest that open theists' redefinition of the future is an attempt to preempt the obvious question they must answer regarding prophecy and nonphysical information.

If the future does not even exist in the form of information, it is ridiculous to attempt a definition if it. We know information is real, and we know it exists independent of any physical medium. But if we follow the logic of open view theologians, there should not be any available information about something that does not exist in concrete form. Information can be disseminated through material things, such as computers, papers, and almost any inanimate or animate object. Information exists, both inside and outside the created order. The reader has probably begun to notice the difficulties of accepting the open view's premise that God cannot have information outside of the created order.

Is it possible for something to exist in this universe that could be outside God's knowledge? Is it possible to say that information can exist outside of God's attribute of omniscience and be independent of it? Open view theologians defend their theology by asserting that they are not really challenging God's knowledge—while doing precisely that. They claim to affirm God's knowledge with a caveat: God knows everything that exists in concrete form. This is code language to limit God's knowledge to created things. However, since information is real and is not a *created thing*, the open view's theological parameters are inadequate to explain a reality that includes information. This could be the reason that none of their proponents have actually addressed the issue of information as a reality outside the physical realm. Open view theologians simply have avoided any discussion on the issue of non-created information.

The Bible states, "The Logos was with God and the Logos was God" (John 1:1). *The Logos* can be translated as the "Word" or "Verb," and it can also be translated as "knowledge." Boyd has suggested that God can only know what has been created.[23] If Boyd's statement is true, then God must have been incapable of knowledge before creation,

---

[23] Boyd, 17.

which is of course a ridiculous assertion. Since every created thing existed in the mind of the creator before it came into being, it is simply not possible to argue that God only knows created things. This is especially true because God conceived the entire universe *before* it came into being. Thus, information preexisted creation, and not the other way around, as open theists appear to suggest.

Openness Reaction Against Determinism

In the introduction of *The God of the Possible,* Boyd stated, "Unfortunately, some people are beginning to toss around the alarmist label of 'heresy.'"[24] This is a preemptive salvo to what Boyd anticipated was going to be a negative reaction to his book. Boyd considered the so-called heresy allegation alarmist. However, the fact remains that open view theologians have pushed the theological envelope to the breaking point in their discussion regarding God's omniscience. While it might be too early to declare the open view as heresy—and the jury is still out on this—further erosion of God's character may actually disfigure the biblical God to the point of becoming unrecognizable.

Since the early Church Fathers, theologians have accepted that God started the clock that marks time. Classical theology has held that God exists outside and independent of time.[25] This is not a controversial concept. God existed before creation (Gen. 1:1). Time did not exist before creation. Therefore, God existed before there was time, which means that God is not confined to either time or creation. Most theologians believe that time—past, present, and future—is instantaneous to God. God's existence outside the confinement of time (his timelessness) implies that people's futures are as real to God as the present is to us. This is precisely openness's main objection. Sanders explained his rejection of God's timelessness thus,

> Our rejection of divine timelessness and our affirmation of dynamic omniscience are the most controversial elements in our proposal and the view of foreknowledge receives the most

---

[24] Boyd, 12.
[25] John Calvin, "Free Will and Predestination," from *Institutes of Christian Religion* (1597), translated by John Allen, 1813.

attention. However, the *watershed issue* in the debate is not whether God has exhaustive definite foreknowledge (EDF) but whether God is ever affected by and responds to what we do. This is the same watershed that divides Calvinism from Arminianism.[26]

In this quote, Sanders pointed to their rejection of God's timelessness as their most controversial. Sanders claimed that God exists in time, but instead of answering the controversy, he moved to the "watershed issue" of how God is affected by human behavior. Sanders tried to deflect attention from their redefinition of God's nature by inserting open theology's emphasis on God's relational aspect with people. Since in open view theology God is affected by human behavior, Sanders stated that God's relational aspect is "the watershed issue" for open theology. That is, everything has to be interpreted through the prism of God's open relationship with humanity. The problem for Sanders is that he has not proven that God does not know the future.

There are two additional problems with Sanders's statement. First, people's relationships with God are not a give-and-take among equals in which both, people and God, are equally influenced by their interactions. Sanders's inference cannot be true for obvious reasons: God is a spirit, and humans are irrevocably created of matter. We do have a spiritual component, but we cannot experience the spiritual world of God in our current form to the same extent that God does. There is simply no human way for us to reach God's realm of existence to influence him from our temporal physical state.

The second problem with Sanders's quote is the assumption that God's response to us when we approach him by faith means that God "is influenced by us." That is, Sanders makes the leap to say that God's responses to our prayers have the result of changing and affecting him. Let me say that people have as much influence on God as fish in a fish tank can influence their owners. The watershed issue for open theism might be the human ability to influence God. However, I believe that the watershed issue in our discussion has to do with the kind of God our Creator is and what he has revealed about himself to people. Sanders brushed over his assertion that God experiences time like people. This

---

[26] John Sanders, Opentheism.info. (Accessed January 2013.)

is not a minor point. God most certainly does not experience time like humans because he is not a human (Num. 23:19).

Open theists have advanced two fundamental premises regarding God's nature: that God exists in time and that, as a result, he cannot know the future. These two basic premises are in direct contradiction to biblical theology. Most theological experts have always held God's timeless existence, which is directly related to his knowledge of the future. Open view theologians claim they are only defining the nature of the future, but in reality, they are redefining the orthodox understanding of God's nature.

John Calvin taught that God not only knows the future but that he decreed every future human action and historical event. In Calvin's theology, the word *decree* is synonymous with *predetermination*. Whatever God knows, he has decreed. And whatever he has decreed is predestined to happen as he has preordained. Most Calvinists would accept the "exhaustively settled future" concept with its accompanying deterministic connotations without any major objections. Since they believe everything is preordained, God does not have foreknowledge per se. God only knows what he has preordained.

Calvin's salvation theology has been summarized with the TULIP acronym.[27] We recognize that this acronym does not do justice to the vast volumes of Calvinistic theological thought and the thought that subsequent theologians have put forth. Nevertheless, TULIP is defined as follows:

> **T—Total Depravity:** Humanity is completely and utterly unable to perform any good works because they are "dead in trespasses and sins."

> **U—Unconditional Election:** God's election of those who would be saved is not dependent on their sins or their ability to repent. God chose those who would be saved according to the pleasure of His will, and the rest He left up to their sinful consequences.

---

[27] David N. Steele and Curtis C. Thomas, *The Five Points of Calvinism* (Phillipsburg, New Jersey: Presbyterian and Reformed Publishing, 1982), 16–19.

L—Limited Atonement: Jesus's death is only intended to be effective for those who God has chosen from the foundation of the world.

I—Irresistible Grace: People cannot resist God's grace. Anyone called will respond to God because God's grace cannot be resisted.

P—Perseverance of the Saints: Those who are called are secured forever regardless of what they do during their lifetimes. This is also called the security of the believers.

Let me point out that I am not a Calvinist, and I do not agree with Calvin's predestination theology for reasons that are beyond the scope of this book. I make mention to Calvinistic theology solely to point out that open theists' main objections are reactions to Calvinism, which is the main reason I believe their conclusions are wrongheaded.

Open theists have several objections to Calvinistic theology I think are valid. Let us share a few. If God has preordained every human thought, act, or event, then (1) people are not truly free, (2) God is the author of evil, (3) prayer is unnecessary, and (4) God is not good. In fact, if God has preordained every human thought and act, it is not possible for humanity to be guilty of sin. Open theists object that, under strict Calvinism, humans do not have self-determination, which is fundamental for moral accountability. However, in order to reach such a conclusion, we have to accept that *foreknowledge, preordination*, and *causality* are synonymous.

An objective reading of Scripture does not support the conclusion that God is responsible for evil or that people are not accountable for their behavior. The open view's language is deceptive on this point. Boyd's explanation of traditional theology equates foreknowledge with determinism. This is the logical conclusion for traditional Calvinism, but while I agree that theological determinism is not a biblical doctrine that properly defines God's impartiality, it is unnecessary to question God's foreknowledge based on Calvinism's error. I hold that *foreknowledge* is not synonymous with *determinism*. Foreknowledge is advanced information. As such, foreknowledge is neutral as it relates to causality and human freewill.

Decrees are intentional and irrevocable decisions made by God independent of any action by the creature. If God decreed that an event would happen, then God's word on those circumstances is final. He will cause the decreed event to take place. Theopedia.com defines *decrees* thus:

> The decrees of God relate to all future things without exception: whatever is done in time, was foreordained before time began. God's purpose was concerned with everything, whether great or small, whether good or evil, although with reference to the latter we must be careful to state that while God is the Orderer and Controller of sin, He is not the Author of it in the same way that He is the Author of good.[28]

Open theists object to this type of definition of God's activity in relationship to humans. While I can sympathize with them in this area, I believe they go too far in their discussion. Instead of showing from Scripture how strict Calvinism might be incompatible with human accountability and with God's impartiality, Boyd jumped into accusations of pagan influence in classical theology.[29] There is no doubt gnostic thought, in the Manichean for, influenced St. Augustine's theology, but I do not believe it is necessary to jump to that subject to oppose determinism.

Open view theologians dismiss the charge they are challenging God's knowledge by claiming that they are only discussing the nature of the future. However, their claim runs against their stated positions—that is, no one can honestly discuss the nature of something that does not exist. Boyd's only alternative is to redefine something that does exist—God's knowledge. In their view, God irrevocably entered into a temporal existence when he created, and thus, God experiences time in the same linear fashion that humans do. By redefining how God experiences time, or by confining God to time, open theists have tried to argue that God's entrance into time precludes his knowledge of the future. This is precisely the point open theists have asserted but have been unable to actually prove. They have no idea what God knows or does not know, and neither does anyone else. Nature and the Bible are

---

[28] "Decrees." Theopedia.com. (Accessed February 2013.)
[29] Boyd, 109.

the only sources of information regarding God's knowledge, and both affirm God's timelessness, and his knowledge of the future (Rom. 1:20; Isaiah 46:10).

The premise asserted by open theism that the future does not exist leads to two logical conclusions. If openness theology is true, then (1) prophecy is impossible, and the prophet Isaiah exaggerated when he declared, writing under the inspiration of the Holy Spirit, that God is different from idols in that he makes the future known or that he knows the end from the beginning (Is. 46:10); and (2) advance information about any future reality is unattainable, contradicting Boyd's own premise that God "has remarkable knowledge about the future of his chosen people."[30] The first conclusion is false according to Scripture. The second conclusion is negated by Boyd's internal contradiction.

Boyd stated that since he came to the conclusion that God does not know the future, he "no longer struggles with the issue of evil as he used to."[31] This is an admirable pursuit, to say the least, but there is no need to reinterpret God's character to appease one's conscience or to refute the false accusation that God is the author of evil. Open theists cannot reconcile the God of foreknowledge with the presence of evil in the world. This is their blind spot. His concern regarding any possible connection between God and evil is understandable. This is an age-old ethical dilemma. Atheists have held for the longest time that the presence of evil in the world is an argument against foreknowledge. I believe this is a non-sequitur because there is no cause and effect relationship between knowledge and evil. Evil is confined to the closed system in which we live, and it can never reach into God's spiritual realm.

As such, evil is the distortion of the created order that affects humanity exclusively, and not a distortion of God's character. The Bible does not allow for the interpretation that God has anything to do with evil on this earth, even though classical theology has affirmed that God decreed evil. But classical theology must teach that God decreed evil because they believe God determined every aspect of the human experience. I believe this is a false conclusion. The reality is that while

---

[30] Boyd, 25.
[31] Ibid, 8.

God has access to the created order, he does not even exist within the creative order to be affected by it.

Open theists also need to find a logical explanation for the dichotomy between God's foreknowledge and people's freewill that is different from the classical view. In their effort to explain away the historical definition of *foreknowledge*, open view theologians have misread or misrepresented the classical view and almost every passage they have presented as evidence, as we shall see later. Open theists have erroneously suggested that foreknowledge necessitates causality or preordination. The fact is that foreknowledge does not require divine action. I agree that whatever God foreknows has to take place the way he knows it, but that is a far cry from saying that he is the cause of the action. The idea that God's foreknowledge makes him the primary causal agent for everything that happens within creation, including the human choice to sin, is not supported in Scripture. Actually, the Bible affirms the opposite (Jam. 1:14–15). One thing is certain, God's impartiality prevents him from holding people responsible for their sins if they do not have actionable free moral agency.

Foundational Presuppositions

The open view has three foundational premises. First, the future does not exist and cannot be known. Second, if the future exists and God knows it, people are not truly free.[32] Open theists find God's foreknowledge to be incompatible with human freewill. Third, if God knows the future, he must also be responsible for evil because he must have decreed it.[33] Open theists also find that God's foreknowledge is incompatible with the existence of evil in the world. Boyd made this point with his Hitler analogy. If God knows the future, he must believe that allowing Hitler's evil was better than not allowing it.[34] Our contention is that biblical revelation does not support open theism's first foundational principle. As a consequence of the falsehood of the first principle, the other two principles are inoperative because they flow from the first. There are two reasons to reject open theism's original

---

[32] Boyd, 123.

[33] Ibid, 99.

[34] Ibid, 99

premise: (1) God exists independently of his creation. Otherwise, he would be confined to it or one with it. (2) God exists outside the limitations of a linear time continuum. He is eternal.

Open theism connects the second foundational principle to the moral consequences of freewill. The affirmation that people have moral freedom is true, as a matter of both revelation and experience. If the garden of Eden account was about anything, it was about the human option to reject God's lordship. I reject openness's second foundational principle because God's foreknowledge, in and of itself, does not negate people's freedom of action and responsibility. Open theists have not been able to make a *cause-and-effect* connection between information and causality. They have not even tried to make such a connection.

Openness theology's third foundational principle attempts to connect God's foreknowledge with evil. We accept the principle that God is good, but open view theologians ask, "How can God be understood as being good while remaining unmoved about his knowledge of human evil?"[35] Boyd asked the question with a preconceived answer built in. His suggestion is that God's goodness is jeopardized because he appears to be unsympathetic to the evil that humans do and experience. Boyd's reasoning goes like this: if God knows the future, he must know the evil that people will do in the future, and since God is not actively doing anything to stop this evil, then he must find redeeming value in evil. God's attitude regarding evil can only mean that he is not good if he has foreknowledge. Boyd would claim that foreknowledge makes God an accomplice with evil.

Open view theologians think they have solved the perceived dilemma by attempting to redefine our common understanding of the future, of reality, and of God's foreknowledge. The open view presents the dilemma in such a way that accepting one position would demand a denial of the other. Hence, open theists' either/or dilemma is shortsighted and incorrect. The issue is not whether God can be good if he knows the future. The issue is whether knowing the future necessarily makes God an accomplice to evil.

This is an artificially created contradiction with the sole purpose of ultimately redefining the classical understanding of foreknowledge.

---

[35] Boyd, 98–99.

Once the dilemma has been presented as a contradiction, open view theologians' only option is to reject the portion of the equation that does not fit their theology. As a result, they reject the aspect of God's character that is least offensive—God's foreknowledge. Surely, no one wants to go down the road of arguing against God's goodness.

Although the logic appears to flow well from the premises, the entire argument rests on faulty presuppositions. The fact that freewill requires that people make decisions without external compulsion does not necessitate a redefinition of God's foreknowledge. Additionally, the presence of sin and evil in the world is not an indictment on God's goodness. Openness theologians redefined God's attributes without providing enough evidence to show that such redefinitions are warranted. The biblical writers do not appear to have any issues regarding the dichotomy of God's foreknowledge and human freewill or about God's goodness and the presence of evil in the world. These are difficult subjects, and we have to be conscientious about addressing them. These dichotomies would be irreconcilable contradictions if people were acting under divine compulsion while being held accountable for their actions by God. The Bible does not support the interpretation that God's foreknowledge has ever served as a weapon against human freewill.

All of God's attributes are absolute, and as such, an argument can be made that any one of them, or all of them, can violate human freedom. For instance, God is almighty. His power is so overwhelming that no human can withstand it. The only thing that prevents God from forcing humanity into acting according to his wishes is his self-imposed restraint. God is omnipresent. As such, his presence in everything we do violates our freedom of action because we are being watched constantly. God is meddling in all our affairs, and he cannot help it. Again, his omnipresence can become an intimidating force that could condition our behavior.

The fact that all of God's attributes could be compulsory by their very nature makes it illogical to isolate foreknowledge as the only attribute that violates human freedom. The same argument presented against foreknowledge is as valid against any other attribute. It can be as easily said that God's omnipotence and omnipresence can have the same controlling effect on people as foreknowledge. If God decided to use any of his attributes against us, there would not be one of us that could do anything about it. God's omnipotence could be more controlling than foreknowledge itself. God certainly has the power, if he so desired to force us to conform to his wishes, but his restraint (his love, grace, and impartiality) prevents him from doing so.

Our moral freedom is God's gift to us, and it would be imprudent to say that God was unaware of the perceived contradiction that it would create for mortals. Our moral freedom, thus, depends on God's grace as expressed through his self-restraint. We are not the victims of God's attributes. On the contrary, we are blessed that God chose to create us free at the expense of the pain we would cause him with our blatant and flagrant rebellion. Even though God can overpower us to act according to his desires, for our sakes, he chooses not to do so. Boyd, for example, protests against the charge that open theists are redefining God's foreknowledge, by claiming that he is presenting a discussion regarding the nature of the future.[36] However, a fair reading of *The God of the Possible*, as well as other open view theologians' writings, leads to the conclusion that what is at stake is God's attribute of knowledge.

Libertarian Freewill

Open theism has adopted the presupposition that God created humanity with "libertarian" freewill.[37] Theopedia.com, the Encyclopedia of Christianity, provides the following description of libertarian freewill.

> Libertarian freewill means that our choices are free from the determination or constraints of human nature and free from any predetermination by God. All "freewill theists" hold that *libertarian freedom* is essential for moral responsibility, for if our choice is determined or caused by anything, including our own desires, they reason, it cannot properly be called a free choice. Libertarian freedom is, therefore, the freedom to act contrary to one's nature, predisposition and greatest desires.

---

[36] Boyd, 15.
[37] William Hasker, "The Incompatibility of Libertarian Free Will and Divine Timelessness." *Theology Today* (Princeton, 1996).

Responsibility, in this view, always means that one could have done otherwise.[38]

According to Hasker, libertarian freewill means that the "agent is free with respect to a given action at a given time if at that time it is within the agent's power to perform the action and also in the agent's power to refrain from the action."[39] The definition is harmless enough as far as it goes, but it is the rationale for deeper theological distortions. When open view theologians speak of a libertarian freewill, they are advancing three basic presuppositions.

First, libertarian freewill has to be absolute in order to guarantee that our relationship with God is voluntary and reciprocal. Second, God cannot know the future of any human action. Such knowledge would rob people of their libertarian freedom, and as a result it would eliminate reciprocity—the concept that our relationship with God is a real give and take between God and humanity. The rationale for rejecting foreknowledge, in this case, is that if God knows something to be true in the future, then it must happen as he knows it. And if it must happen as God already knows it, then people are not truly free to choose. This assertion is based on the error that information is causative, which is not. Third, if individuals are not free to make their own moral choices, then God cannot hold them accountable for their sins.

Open view theologians make an insurmountable leap in logic when they assume a direct correlation between human free moral agency and God's cognitive attribute. These two apparently competing realities are not necessarily contradictory because they are not related, and they do not even function in the same realm. I hold that God's impartiality functions as a restraint to his power, and this restraint is the only guarantor for human freedom and for everything we do. The limitations of the creature and the awesomeness of all of God's attributes require that God be the one exercising restraint. His restraint can be seen, for example, in Jesus's words, he "sends rain on the just and on the unjust." (Matt. 5:45). God created the climate in such a way that both the just and the unjust benefit to the same extent. In this way, God's impartiality is demonstrated to everyone at the same time. God's

---

[38] "Libertarian free will." Theopedia.com. (Accessed January 2012.)

[39] William Hasker, *The Openness of God: A Biblical Challenge to the Traditional Understanding of God* (Downers Grove, IL: InterVarsity Press, 1994), 136–137.

impartiality is already built into the system. If we accept Hasker's definition of *libertarian freewill,* we have to conclude that libertarian freewill has to restrict God's omniscience because human freewill is absolute.

The definition of freewill as an absolute human attribute leads open theists to present three philosophical presuppositions that are contingent upon one another, resulting in circular reasoning. First, a reciprocal relationship between God and humanity is not possible without libertarian freewill. This would be true if God's knowledge were causative. However, open theism does not offer a compelling theological case for this option because its proponents do not even address the issue of information as a noncausative reality.

Second, once open theists established the incompatibility suggested in the first premise, they jump to the unsupported conclusion that libertarian freewill is incompatible with God's foreknowledge. This is the logical progression: (a) freewill and foreknowledge are incompatible, as open theists have proposed, and (b) since we know experientially that people have libertarian freewill, (c) it follows that God's foreknowledge, as described by the classical view, must not be true. Open theists have chosen to redefine God's foreknowledge instead of adjusting their definition of libertarian freewill.

Finally, as a result of the first two premises, the logical conclusion is that God's omniscience is limited to the present time. How does anyone know this? Open theists make their gravest mistake when they propose that libertarian freewill necessarily limits God's foreknowledge. They assume, incorrectly, that our moral decision-making freedom is normative and can be projected onto God. This must also mean that a normative principle for humanity has a direct correlation to God's character. While God's character is revealed in nature and through nature, any normative principle proceeds from God and not from human experience (Rom. 1:19–20). The Bible actually assumes that God's impartiality is the normative principle for God's character, not libertarian freewill.

The Issue of Information

Open view theologians do not discuss the all-important subject of information as a discipline in and of itself. Information exists independently of concrete reality. For instance, every human invention existed in the mind of an inventor before it became a reality. Thomas Edison had a concept of the light bulb before he created the first one. Henry Ford visualized the T-Model before the first truck hit the road.

The fact that information exists in a nonphysical realm provides the rationale for understanding how God knows the future without the rigid interpretation of the preordination of historical facts. For example, the phrase "God is love" could be contained in a computer disk, in a person's mind, on a piece of paper, or it could be carved on a tree. Each medium has the information about God's love, but the information itself is not intrinsically bound to any of those physical items. Any person who comes in contact with any of these mediums of communication could acquire the same information. The person does not have to take the computer disk home or cut down the tree to acquire the information. The statement "God is love" is true regardless of the medium that is used to communicate it. The statement has intrinsic value within itself. What is more remarkable about information is that once the person has received it, it can be safely stored in the person's mind forever, even if it never becomes a concrete reality.

Information, then, exists independently of the item that contains it. God has nonhistorical information (in that the events have not happened) and nonphysical information (in that God has not used a physical medium to communicate his message) about the future, but he has information that allows him to make the future known. Not only that, but anyone who comes in contact with God's revelation of the future can acquire the same information. However, having the information does not, in and of itself, necessitate the conclusion that God is the causal agent for all human thought and behavior. God's foreknowledge cannot be considered compulsory as it relates to human behavior because it exists as information in a nonphysical realm, not as a concrete historical reality.

God and Time

The concepts of past, present, and future have meaning only as they relate to the fact that time began when God sent the universe into motion. And we can only understand time because we are confined to it. Similarly, the word *foreknowledge* has meaning only as it relates to humanity's concept of time. That is, anything behind the present time is the past, and anything ahead of the present time is the future. But God does not have foreknowledge, per se. He simply knows. He knows the totality of time because he is the "Alpha and the Omega, the first and the last, the beginning and the end" (Rev. 22:13). The eternal Logos of God is not limited by time or is confined to it.

Our existence is strictly defined within the limits of time and space, and nothing that existed before creation—or outside the known universe—can be fully grasped or understood by us. The inescapable fact is that we cannot reach beyond our human boundaries. Before creation, the concepts of past, present, and future had absolutely no meaning. If God was not restricted by time before creation, he could not have become restricted by time after his own creation. This would be analogous to saying that Bill Gates was able to think for himself before he created Microsoft, but after he created his computer operating system, he lost his independent thinking capacity.

Time is a by-product of God's creative activity and not a precursor of it. Therefore, time, which is an abstract concept directly related to the fact that God started the universe's clock with his creative activity, has no bearing on God's existence, and it cannot have any bearing on his ability to know everything and anything within his created universe. Time is not a part of, and is not connected to, God's existence; this should be evident enough because God existed eternally before creation. God experiences all things as an eternal (timeless) present because his knowledge is instantaneous. "With the Lord one day is like a thousand years" (2 Pet. 3:8). That is, time makes no difference to God.

Is it possible for God to create a reality in which he loses the capacity to know everything contained therein? This would be analogous to the fallacious philosophical question that asks if God is omnipotent, can he create a rock so big that he cannot lift? This is a dumb question couched in philosophical jargon because everyone knows or should know that no sentient being can create anything outside his nature. The fact that God foreknows the end from the beginning does not mean that he is the direct causal force of events that take place within his created order, as the open view suggests. On the contrary, it means that God has exhaustive information of everything leading to the end and everything in between. He has foreknowledge of all of the events related to history's progression from the beginning because time plays no role in his ability to know. God knows how the game is played and how it ends.

Understanding Foreknowledge

Historically, there are two basic perspectives in understanding the concept of God's foreknowledge: the "classical view" and the "open view."[40] The classical view proposes that the future is "exhaustively settled"[41] because God has predetermined all the aspects of its outcome. Boyd adds that if the future is settled, then people are not truly free because they are not able to change their own futures. The fallacy of this argument is two-fold.

First, since people do not live in the future, there is nothing people can do to change a nonexistent future for them, regardless of what God knows. The future exists in God's mind in the form of exhaustive, noncausal information, as mentioned earlier. Open theists interpret the classical view as a fatalistic, deterministic system of theology, which it is. That is, theological determinism teaches that God has preordained every aspect of human conduct and actions, to even include the movement of specs of dusts from the ground. Classical proponents will accept the preordination of life but reject the fatalistic label, which it does not make sense, but that's their prerogative.

Second, the phrase "exhaustively settled future" assumes that the settled-ness of the future is in historical facts. This is such an amateurish error that it's hard to define. There is nothing that exists in God's mind in the form of information that can be construed as

---

[40] Boyd, 8.
[41] Ibid.

historically real as it relates to human history. For instance, the apostle Paul said; "If then you have been raised with Christ, seek the things that are above, where Christ is, seated at the right hand of God" (Col. 3:1). As far as God's knowledge is concerned, believers in Christ are already "raised with Christ." And yet, we are still waiting for the day in which the resurrection will become a historical reality. Information regarding the future reality of our resurrection does not imply the settled-ness of that reality as a historical fact. This is an error for both, Calvinism and open theists for defining their concepts based on a flawed deterministic position.

The issue is not weather God knows the future. The real issue is whether God's knowledge of the future is determinative for human behavior in the present. I argue that it is not, while classical theologians argue that that it is, and open view proponents reject the deterministic definition as if these were the only two options. Boyd described the future as "open ended and that God knows it as such."[42] Additionally, Boyd stated that God knows the future "as a realm of possibilities."[43] Let us examine these concepts.

The Open-Ended Future

Open theists believe that God's decision to grant freewill to humanity inherently limits God's knowledge of future human behavior. They argue that in order for humans to be truly free, God cannot know ahead of time the future choices of free moral agents. The contention is that if God foreknows future human choices, then that knowledge by necessity negates true human freedom. The reason cited is that anything God knows exhaustively must come to pass exactly as he knows it. This truth is obvious enough—anything God knows about anything must be exhaustively true. Again, open theists make the mistake of designing their theology in a vacuum. They completely ignore that information exists in a realm independent of the physical world, and it does not determine physical events unless the possessor of such knowledge decided to use it to control the outcomes of human decisions.

---

[42] Boyd, 15.
[43] Ibid.

Openness theologians have not considered the possibility that God's knowledge of the future is not necessarily determinative, and if they have, they have not presented any discussions regarding this essential subject. If we can show that having advanced knowledge is not determinative, then people retain their freedom and the rationale for open theism collapses. They have also appeared to suggest that in order for people to be free, future human activity must be random and unpredictable to God. Additionally, Boyd has stated that if God does not allow for contradictory human choices to be made in the future, humanity's freedom is an illusion.[44] There are at least three problems with this reasoning.

First, human freedom cannot be defined based on the randomness of events to God. As long as the events are random to people, that is, as long as those events were not predesigned and predetermined, our moral freedom is not in jeopardy. Second, people make contradictory choices all the time in the present, but there is no evidence that God's knowledge of those choices in the present has stopped anyone from making them. Third, people cannot make contradictory choices in their own futures because they do not live there. People never make decisions about the future in the future. All of our decisions are made in the present. Therefore, it is not possible to argue with credibility that God's foreknowledge prevents us from changing future decisions when we can never make decisions in the future. However, if openness theologians were able to argue, convincingly, that God's present knowledge prevents us from making free choices in the present, then they would be onto something.

There is at least one additional problem with the concept that people should be able to change their futures. People are free to make contradictory choices at any time they want, but people cannot make contradictory choices in the future. Whatever contradictory choices people are able to make, they have to make them in the present. Our lives are irrevocably tied to the present. It is experientially true that people change their minds all the time. However, we need to note that God does not function as a coercive agent for human behavior in the present. The same is true about the future. God's knowledge is not

---

[44] Boys, 135.

coercive, and people retain the freedom to make their moral choices regardless of God's knowledge. Thus, if God's knowledge of the future strips people from their freedom in the future, then, it necessarily follows that God's knowledge of the present also takes away freewill.

People's ability to make decisions is based on the information they have at the time the decisions are made, not based on anything God may or may not know about said decisions. Human freedom is safeguarded by God's impartiality and not by his ignorance. It is not accurate to say that human volition is restricted as a result of any information that God has. Whatever restrictions we may have in our decision-making process are the result of our finite capacity to know and the physical limitations inherent within our natures.

One perspective within the open view holds that God knows the future but has chosen to restrict his knowledge of it to ensure human freedom.[45] I cannot even imagine how someone can actually believe that an all-knowing God can stop himself from knowing something he already knows, but to each its own. In order for God to restrict his knowledge of anything, he must change his very nature, which is, of course, impossible. The suggestion that God can choose not to know something he already knows is incongruent, at best. I suggest that God safeguards humanity's freedom through self-restraint to unleash all his power against us, and not by unknowing information he already knows. God's self-control is the vehicle God uses to put in check his awesome power to protect human freedom. God's knowledge of Adam and Eve's disobedience did not prevent them from rebelling. If there was a time that God's knowledge could have prevented human behavior, the Garden of Eden was the perfect time. God didn't, and Adam was free to disobey.

Redefining Foreknowledge

Open theism is unsustainable without first redefining God's attribute of foreknowledge. One of its basic unstated premises appears to be that since the future is hidden to us, it must also be hidden to God.

---

[45] Christian Research Apologetics and Ministry, "*What Is Open Theism?*" http://www.carm.org, 2003. (Accessed March 2011.)

This is an argument that is made from silence. There is not one open theist who knows the extent of God's knowledge about the future or about anything else, for that matter. I affirm God's foreknowledge because the Bible appears to be fairly clear that God knows the end from the beginning.

Open theists must establish the extent to which they know the limits of God's knowledge if they pretend to redefine his attributes. That is, unless they know God's cognitive limitations regarding people's futures, their argument falls short. I get the basic argument—people have to be free in fact in order for God to hold them accountable for their actions. The problem with the argument is that foreknowledge is not a factual infringement on volition. In the attempt to redefine God's omniscience, open theists leave the impression that God's knowledge is dependent on humanity's ability to create "the whole of reality."[46] This is simply not a credible argument. When open view theologians suggest that God's knowledge of human activity cannot extend beyond the present, they are not just defining the nature of the future. They are redefining the omniscient attributes of the Creator. Their conclusions make the Creator's knowledge subservient to the creature's creative activity.

Let us agree that people can create their own historical reality. However, it is a far cry to say that people are able to create the whole of reality. If this is true, then we must also agree that God has the power and wisdom to create his own eternal reality, which includes humanity's reality. The Bible declares that he knows "the end from the beginning" (Is. 46:10). I suggest that God's knowledge of the whole of his reality has to include humanity's future. When the Bible affirms that God "knows the end from the beginning," it is strictly making reference to people's destinies and not to the rock formations on Mars. The phrase "the end from the beginning" can only be made in reference to God's relationship to people's linear experience of time on this earth. The phrase can only mean that God has known the totality of human history since before he set the universe in motion.

Let me conclude by stating that since God is eternal and he existed before time was created, his knowledge of the "end from the

---

[46] Boyd, 17.

beginning" is not limited or restricted by any human action. Our future resides outside of our grasp because we are temporal beings by design and nature. People's lives are distinctively marked by a beginning and by an ending. The Bible establishes that humanity's days on this earth are counted (Job 14:5). But God does not have a beginning or an ending (Ps. 90:2). Rather, God establishes both the beginning and the ending for creation and his creatures. Thus, if God established the beginning (and no one disputes this), and the ending (God has claimed to have done this), that means that God knows both ends of the spectrum of human life.

God is the eternal I AM. In his infinite wisdom, the eternal I AM created people to live in the present, so they could relate to him from their persistent present. Yesterday is gone, and tomorrow may never come. But we can always find God today. People need to understand that when we speak of God's "future," it is for our benefit because God does not have a future per se. We can experience God only in a persistent present time.

The Issue of Unintended Consequences

God's ability to predict the future should not be in dispute, but it is. Even though the Bible is filled with prophetic utterances, open theists insist that God cannot know the future. Foreknowledge is the essential element for prophecy, and it is intrinsic to God's fundamental character. Otherwise, prophecy would not be possible. Please indulge me one more time: the terms *foreknowledge* and *prophecy* have meaning insofar as we speak of humans' relationship to time. Both terms relate to the human future, a future we cannot know but that God has said he "makes known." It is disheartening that open theists can dismiss God's knowledge so cavalierly.

Hasker has suggested that God assumed a temporalness that prevents him from knowing the future.[47] Hasker's logic is difficult to follow on this point because he does not take his premise to its logical conclusion. It appears that Hasker has proposed that God exists with the dichotomy of being eternal and temporal at the same time. This is based

---

[47] Hasker, *The Openness of God*, 128.

on the illogical proposition that two contradictory and opposite qualities can coexist in the perfect God of the universe. People can hold contradictory beliefs, mostly because we are not always able to appreciate the complexity of the issues. Since God has complementary attributes, he cannot have any two attributes that contradict each other. Allow me to discuss two types of dichotomies to clarify Hasker's point.

The first type of dichotomy has to do with God's essence as a Spirit and his relationship to creation. The Bible teaches that God is both transcendent and immanent. When Solomon was dedicating the temple, he stated, "But will God really dwell on earth? The heavens, even the highest heaven, cannot contain you. How much less this temple I have built!" (1 Kgs. 8:27). He is transcendent in that he exists independently and outside of the created order. According to Solomon, the heavens "cannot contain" him. God created the universe, but he did not become an integral part of the universe in the process. This is one of the main reasons we reject all the pantheistic religions. God is not one with the universe, and he is not part of the universe. He transcends the universe.

However, God is also immanent in that he is free to interact with his own creation. The angel of the Lord, who is understood by most theologians as a physical manifestation of Jesus, appeared to many saints in the Old Testament (Ex. 3:2, Judg. 6:11, etc.). These appearances are called a theophanies. That is, God created the universe with such properties that, if he chose, he could enter it at will. Jesus is the primary example of this principle (Matt. 1:18–25). Jesus, the eternal Son of God, entered the world and dwelled among us. The transcendent God became immanent when Jesus was born of a virgin. God's transcendence and immanence can coexist within the divine essence because the triune God, by becoming immanent, does not surrender his transcendence. Therefore, immanence and transcendence are not contradictory attributes within the Godhead. God retained his transcendence—the Father and the Holy Spirit remained in their eternal habitation—while becoming immanent in Jesus when the Son took upon himself human form.

A second type of dichotomy deals with irrevocably contradictory elements. Let's take an example from God's character. The Bible reveals God's moral character as good (Ezra 8:22, Ps. 73:1, Mk. 10:18). The Bible also teaches that evil has entered God's created world. One of the most basic definitions of *evil* is "the absence of good."[48] Unlike transcendence and immanence, God cannot be good and evil at the same time. He cannot be good and at the same time have the absence of good. He cannot be half-good and half-evil. Jesus affirmed this principle when he stated that a "kingdom divided against itself is laid waste, and no city or house divided against itself will stand" (Matt. 12:15). In the same way that Jesus cannot cast out demons with the power of demons, God cannot be good and evil at the same time.

God's transcendence and immanence coexist as complementary attributes because they do not represent contradictory aspects of God's character. Not so with good and evil. Good and evil are inherently contradictory and cannot coexist at the same time in the character of a good God. Jesus used the "day and night" metaphor to illustrate the contrast between good and evil. It is impossible for God to be of the day and the night at the same time (1 Thess. 5:5).

Hasker's claim that God exists as both temporal and eternal belongs to the second type of dichotomy. God can enter the temporal and interact with the temporal, but God cannot *become* temporal in his essence. For God to become temporal means that, after creation, God either had a new beginning or will experience an ending. Temporality is a reference to things confined to and defined by time. God's eternal quality is inherent to who he is. And even in the person of Jesus, God did not become temporal. In Jesus, God *entered* the temporal, but Jesus never *became* temporal in his essence. That was John's point in John 1:1— "In the beginning was the Word and the Word was with God and the Word was God." The eternal word became flesh and dwelled among people, but at no time did the Logos become temporal in the sense that the eternal Logos had a beginning or an ending, even if Jesus the man did.

Therefore, God's eternal attribute is incompatible with a temporal existence. His transcendence and immanence are made possible by his Triune existence. As the creator, his creation is separate and distinct from his person but not alien to him. He can, then, relate to his creation from without and from within. However, God's eternality is intrinsic to his person in the same way that his goodness is. Before

---

[48] Augustine of Hippo. The City of God, XI, Chapter 9.

creation, God was neither transcendent nor immanent. He simply was. However, God was both good and eternal before creation. Thus, creation could not have changed his essence. While God can enter the temporal, he retains his eternal quality and never becomes temporal. Even Jesus, while in the flesh claimed to be the eternal I AM. He said to the Pharisees, "before Abraham was, I am" (John 8:58). Hasker's argument regarding the temporalness of God is not theologically or logically sustainable.

Everything we know about God points to his awesome creative and design abilities. It is foolish to think that God designed his creation with a built-in mechanism that could block his ability to exercise his sovereign power over it. It is not reassuring to consider that upon creating the present system, God surrendered one of his eternal attributes. This is not a small matter. If the universe has unintended consequences to God, then he does not have perfect knowledge.

Open theists can offer the Fall at the garden of Eden as an example of unintended consequences for God. Since open view theologians hold that human decisions have consistently frustrated God's plans, what event could be more frustrating than humanity's full-blown rejection of God at the very beginning of the life experiment on earth? Their implication is clear—God was not fully prepared to deal with human rebellion at the Garden of Eden. It was not a very reassuring chain of events. Even when people create an object, they are careful to identify as many potential problems as possible to avoid unpleasant surprises. If people can be clever enough to identify potential downfalls of their inventions, how much truer should this be about a God who has exhaustive knowledge?

All human inventions have unintended consequences to us for two basic reasons. First, unintended consequences are the result of the limited human capacity to anticipate the unlimited number of external factors that influence the invention. Second, people's finite ingenuity restricts the number of preventive mechanisms they can build into the invention. This cannot be true of God. If God has perfect knowledge, then he must have settled every variable associated with human freewill before he created people.

Un-sustained Presuppositions

Openness theologians described the God of foreknowledge as an evil tyrant that intentionally created some people with the express purpose of sending them to hell. Boyd asks, "If God is eternally certain that various individuals will end up being eternally damned, why does he go ahead and create them?"[49] This is the type of question that unbelievers and atheists ask about God. The open view offers a simple answer to this question. Either the God of foreknowledge is evil, or the traditional view of God's foreknowledge is in error. In light of this dilemma, open view theologians have chosen the lesser of two evils, and thus, they have rejected the classical view of foreknowledge. The open view is more about the nature of God's foreknowledge and how he relates to the undeniable realities of evil and freewill than it is about the nature of the future.

In order to reject the traditional definition of God's foreknowledge, openness theologians must first establish at least two unsubstantiated presuppositions. The first implies that God's ability to know is connected to human creative activity. Since human existence is irrevocably tied to the present, then God's knowledge must also be tied to the present. This presupposition is obviously false. The Bible makes clear that God is able to predict future events in which people are inevitably involved. Human actions cannot determine or limit God's knowledge because he had knowledge before humans entered the stage. And God's knowledge cannot hinder our decision-making process because knowledge is neither causative nor compulsory.

The second presupposition suggests that God's reality is not greater than human reality. While this argument can be made, it is not likely that God experiences *life* the same way that people do. God's reality extends to greater depth than anything the human mind can ever conceive. Humanity is confined to this globe, and regardless of how much we try, we will never comprehend the totality of God's immensity. Human knowledge of the *whole of reality* is limited and deficient because we do not even have exhaustive knowledge of all of our present circumstances. God, on the other hand, has exhaustive knowledge of his whole of reality. By definition, God's whole of reality must include the

---

[49] Boyd, 10.

whole of human experience—past, present and future—because time plays no role in God's ability to know, and he has set the parameters of our existence. If God does not know our futures, then God's declaration that he knows the end from the beginning is false.

For example, the Bible speaks of "the man of lawlessness," or the antichrist (2 Thess. 2:3). The antichrist opposes anything that has to do with Christ and his church. God has predicted that this man will come at the end of the age. The coming of the antichrist is clearly a human event. How could the God of open theism predict more than two thousand years ago that such a man would appear on earth? Daniel spoke of him as the heir of the Roman Empire (Dan. 9:26–27). At the very least, these remarkable prophecies speak to a divine reality that extends beyond the present.

If the readers accept the two basic presuppositions in openness theology, then they can accept the fallacy that the whole of reality does not include humanity's future. However, after our discussion, we have to conclude that God's whole of reality is greater than people's and that it includes future human events. We cannot even fathom what God's knowledge of the whole of reality entails, and to suggest that open theists have unlocked this mystery is to presume too much.

Open theists agree that humanity's future cannot even exist in God's mind because it is not there to be known. In his discussion regarding Isaiah 48, Boyd equates the future "settled in reality" with "settled in God's mind." I don't have a particular opposition to this statement, as far as it goes. But Boyd additionally declared that God's knowledge of the future is confined to what he has purposed for himself.[50] This second assertion is nowhere to be found in Isaiah 48.

Our issue is not whether God knows what he will do. Even we know what we want to do. But, if all God knows is what he has purposed about himself, then he should not be in the business of making prophecies and answering prayers that necessarily include future human activity. Present human behavior sets a path for future consequences and results. From a human perspective, this path does not lead to certain consequences ten, twenty, or one hundred years from now. Humans cannot guess their futures that far ahead. Openness theologians say that

---

[50] Boyd, 30.

neither can God. As we will see shortly, open theism fails the prophecy test, which requires knowledge of the future.

The "God Regrets" Issue

Open theists have stated on different occasions that God has actually regretted some of his actions, such as Saul's selection as Israel's king.[51] We need to clarify that whatever the word *regret* might have meant to God, it could not have meant that he came to the realization that he had made a mistake. God cannot admit to making dumb decisions about human behavior and remain the wise God.[52] This is akin to saying that God can make mistakes and still remain mistake-free. A regret by its very definition is a negative reaction to a hindsight evaluation of past erroneous actions. People look back at their decisions and, after evaluating their results, they have a fresh perspective regarding those decisions.

It is not possible for God to have regrets about his own decisions. He would be second-guessing himself. Forgive me if I do not buy into the openness logic here. It is simply not credible to assert that God has reviewed his past decisions and found them wanting. Whatever Saul's event means, it cannot mean that God was admitting error. A different option must be available.

Saul's rejection is found in 1 Samuel 15. God had given Saul a command to destroy the Amalekites completely, but "Saul and the people chose to spare king Agag" (1 Sam. 15:9). This was an act of willful disobedience by Saul. As a result of his disobedience, God spoke again to Samuel and said, "'I regret that I have made Saul king, for he has turned back from following me and has not performed my commandments.' And Samuel was angry, and he cried to the LORD all night" (1 Sam. 15:11 ESV). The translators used the same translation for 1 Samuel 15:9 that they used in Genesis 6:7 when the Lord "regretted" creating people. The point here is that the term *regrets* suggests that the Lord was deeply concerned—or, as H.V.D. Parunak

---

[51] Boyd, 56–57.
[52] Ibid, 57.

asserted, God "suffered emotional pain—regarding choices Saul made of his own volition."[53]

As a matter of application, God knew that Saul would disobey. The question that someone may ask is, "If God knew Saul would disobey, why would he give him the command to destroy the Amalekites?" The answer is not complicated. Saul, as many Christians today, needed to have his true character revealed. God knew what his true character looked like, and he was not going to entrust the lineage of the Messiah to an unworthy man. But why would God choose Saul as king in the first place? I believe God had to choose Saul for two reasons.

First, God answered the people's demands, and God always deals with us from the perspective of the present. That is, God answered the people to show their foolishness and to reveal the type of man he wanted as king. Second, David was too young and not ready to become king. As a result, the Lord allowed an intermediary to occupy the throne until David was ready.

In the same way that God tested Saul's character to prove his worthiness as king, God will test our characters until one of two things happens: we grow to become more intimate with God, or we expose ourselves as frauds. God was not surprised by Saul's disobedience. God simply exposed something he already knew about Saul's character—the first king of Israel was an unreliable man, and God was not going to deposit the redemption plan for humanity into his lineage.

The point here is that God was not "regretting" Saul's kingship in the sense that he needed to correct a mistake. God was experiencing emotional pain as a result of Saul's decision. God was grieved about rejecting Saul in the same manner that he grieved during the times of Noah, and as he grieves when people today rejects his gracious salvation gift, because his heart always breaks when people reject him. This is his nature as a loving God. Let me make an important point: God loved Saul exactly like he loved David, but when Saul disobeyed, he broke God's heart. This is not different than what happens when people reject him

---

[53] R. D. Bergen, *Vol. 7: 1, 2 Samuel* (electronic ed.). (Nashville: Broadman & Holman Publishers, 2001).

today—God is grieved by the disobedience of each and every one of his creatures.

"A Realm of Possibilities"

Boyd has stated that God knows "[the future] as a realm of possibilities, not certainties."[54] This statement is very confusing because to know the future as possibilities is not to know the future at all. For instance, I know hundreds of possibilities about tomorrow. Actually, if I apply myself, I can know thousands of possibilities. However, it would be a wild stretch to declare that I *know* the future. In Boyd's theology, God's knowledge of the future is so general that he really does not know anything about the future. The best thing the God of openness can do is take educated guesses. This is really disheartening.

Let me illustrate this point. Let us suppose that an airplane is scheduled to land in Atlanta at 5:00 p.m. on Monday. The realm of possibilities for the flight includes at least the following options: (1) the plane can arrive right on time, (2) it can be delayed, (3) it can be hijacked, or (4) it can crash. Does the fact that I know of all these possibilities mean that I know what will actually happen to the plane on Monday? Actually, knowing all the possibilities regarding the flight schedule means that I have a good imagination, but it says nothing about my knowledge about the plane's future. Similarly, the statement that God knows all future possibilities, in reality, says that he does not know anything about the future. Open view theologians need to come up with a better argument.

The "Partly Settled Future" Concept

The partly settled future concept is the most incoherent exposition in *The God of the Possible*. Boyd defines the concept thus: "God predestined and foreknows as settled whatever he sees fit to predestine and foreknow as settled."[55]

---

[54] Boyd, 15.
[55] Ibid, 53.

Since the open view has already established that God cannot know future human activity because those actions have not been created and they do not exist to be known, the previous affirmation by open theists makes it logically impossible, even within open view theology, for God to partly settle any future event that includes uncreated human activity. Boyd cannot expect anyone to accept the contradictory concept of God's ability to partly settle a nonexistent future. If the future does not exist, God cannot partly settle anything in it related to human activity, regardless of how cleverly is defined. Boyd is trying to have it both ways.

First, he made the absolute statement that the future does not exist. Then, he stated that God can predestine and partly settle parts of the future. So, which is it? Does the future exist or not? If the future does not exist, then God has no business settling anything in the future that relates to human activity. Conversely, if the future exists, then, it is within God's purview to know it.

The readers should know that if God cannot know uncreated future events, then it would naturally follow that he cannot partly settle any future human activity. Or, said in another way, even the God of the possible cannot settle that which does not exist. The God of the open view cannot see fit to predict or reveal events he cannot know. His revelation of humanity's future must depend on his knowledge of the future. Otherwise, he is only guessing and putting his reputation and us at risk. To speak of a partly settled future after categorically stating that the future does not exist is to speak out of both sides of the theological mouth.

The partly settled future contradiction is an attempt to resolve the prophecy issue.[56] The question, "How can the God of the open future predict and settle any part of a future He cannot possibly know?" remains unanswered. I hope open view theologians are not suggesting that God's ability to predict the future is based on what might be called educated guesses.

Educated guesses do not satisfy the prophetical test described in Deuteronomy 18:22: "If what a prophet proclaims in the name of the LORD does not take place or come true, that is a message the LORD

---

[56] Boyd, 32–33.

has not spoken." Anybody can make guesses about the immediate future but making predictions about human events that will take place more than a thousand years in the future—well, that is another matter altogether. This is my point: God knows what will happen hundreds and even thousands of years ahead of time, and the partly settled future concept is not adequate to explain the trillions upon trillions of variables that can trip up the best laid out plans.

The Uncreated Future

Open theists want to fit biblical revelation within the *a priori* theological hypothesis that uncreated future events reside outside of God's scope of knowledge. The key word here is *uncreated*. It is not possible to separate uncreated events from God's imagination. Since time is instantaneous to God, he moves from conception to creation instantaneously. Even human experience demonstrates that people conceive their own creations in their minds before they see them in reality. God has an even greater capacity to move from thought to creation. He conceived his creation plan before it became a concrete fact; thus, God can *visualize* uncreated things.

It is inaccurate, therefore, to say that *uncreated* events do not exist in people's minds. If people can visualize their own creations before they become reality, then God must be able do the same thing to an even greater extent. God visualized the universe, and everything contained in it, in eternity past. Humans have the capacity to design, plan, and project future events without actually experiencing them. While it is true that future plans could exist only in our minds, the process leading to the decisions can be experienced as very real. The difference is that humans cannot know the future as certain, only as possibilities, while God has declared that his knowledge of the future is certain.

The biggest difference between God and us is that we can imagine the future but cannot be assured of its coming to pass because we cannot account for all the variables that influence events. God, however, sees the future with absolute certainty because not one of the variables escapes him. If people have the mental capacity to imagine uncreated future decisions, why should we limit an all-knowing God's capacity to visualize the future of his creation to include human events?

Conclusion

God designed and created people with freewill while retaining his sovereignty over creation. God's sovereignty is not in doubt in this discussion. The differences between the open view and traditional theology are deeper than just a difference of opinions regarding God's knowledge. Open theists teach, as we saw with Boyd's examples, that God suffers from the same frailties and dysfunctions as the creature. They view God's foreknowledge as incompatible with freewill mostly because they understand foreknowledge as being causative or determinative. I disagree. Foreknowledge could be incompatible with freewill only if knowledge was causative or coercive. It is neither. According to open theists, foreknowledge, by necessity, makes God the creator of evil by eliminating human volition and responsibility. Again, I disagree. Only deterministic foreknowledge eliminates freewill, and by default makes God the creator of evil. I understand Boyd is arguing against theological determinism. But his error is to base his arguments on foreknowledge. I believe the error is to base the disagreement on the false premise that determinism is a biblical doctrine. Based on God's impartiality, determinism cannot be true.

On the surface, it appears that human freewill and God's foreknowledge are competing principles that cannot logically coexist. This is the wrong battle. I agree that freewill cannot exist in a determined world, but information, as we have argued, is neither compulsory or determinative, and as such, it cannot infringe on human volition. The simplest explanation is that God exists in a domain totally different from humanity, and, as such, the two principles are not inherently contradictory because they do not intersect in real time. That is, God knows everything and as long as his knowledge is not determinative human freewill is protected. Any information God has from his domain cannot have a necessary or causal effect on human volition on earth. Conversely, the opposite is also true: human actions cannot have any direct or indirect influence on God's person. The issue is not whether proponents of the open view have found a solution to the apparent contradiction. They have not. The issue is whether the open view has sacrificed God's knowledge and timelessness at the altar of human freedom for the sole purpose of rejecting theological determinism.

Let me close this chapter with one final observation. People have not unlocked the secret that reconciles human freewill with God's foreknowledge because they have, until now, approached the problem from a deterministic perspective. Human freewill exists within the closed biological system we call the earth and people can make choices, within that system, without God's interference. God has foreknowledge in the form of exhaustive non-causal information from outside the system. This information does not have a compulsory effect on human volition or behavior unless God specifically chooses to exercise his sovereign prerogative to influence circumstances.

The teaching of the wise is a fountain of life.
—Proverbs 13:14, NASB

Chapter TWO
Fallacies, Fallacies, Fallacies

During my freshman year in college, my humanities professor—who claimed to be an atheist—asked the following hypothetical question to the class: "If God is omnipotent, can he create a rock so big that he cannot lift?" Most of the students were confused. We could not answer her logical fallacy. She asked the question banking on the students' ignorance regarding God's nature. The professor's question was based on at least one erroneous assumption, which is, that any amateur theologian knows that God cannot function outside of his nature.

If a creation cannot be greater than its creator, then it follows that her question violated natural order. God, by his very nature, cannot create anything greater than himself, even though he remains omnipotent to always act without restriction to accomplish everything he sets out to do. The professor's question was a logical fallacy dressed up in a false sense of wisdom. It was not a serious challenge to God's existence. Rather, it was an expression of the professor's belief in her own shallow superiority over her freshman class.

In this chapter, we will discuss four examples Boyd gave in support of open theism. However, before we engage the examples, we need to define the terms used regarding the usefulness of metaphorical stories and ethical dilemmas. Metaphors and ethical dilemmas generally do not generate comprehensive studies that produce reliable principles. At best, they yield incomplete inferences. Metaphors and ethical dilemmas need to be accompanied by external evidence if they are going to have a wider application. They have some value to illustrate the points of a given principle, but their usefulness is often overestimated.

In this chapter, I will discuss the role Boyd's examples play in open theism's hermeneutics. While they are not exhaustive examples, they are representative of the theological and philosophical reasoning Boyd uses to defend open theism. They are a different version of my humanities professor's question. They are logical fallacies in that they do not accomplish their intended purpose—to prove that open theism is a viable theological option.

The Ethical Dilemma Fallacy

A friend comes to your house in a state of panic and tells you that an ax murderer is following him. Your friend has blood on him, and he tells you that the ax murderer has killed his family. You let your friend in, and a few minutes later the ax murderer shows up at your door. What will you do? Will you tell him that your friend is in the house and violate the moral absolute against murder by becoming an accessory to your friend's death? Or will you tell the ax murderer that you have not seen your friend to protect his life and violate the moral imperative against lying?

This type of ethical dilemma is intended to force the person to make a decision between two compelling moral imperatives: to protect the sanctity of human life or to protect the need to tell the truth. The real agenda for this and other ethical dilemmas is to give legitimacy to a morally relative decision-making process. That is, the person has to choose between the lesser of two evils. Is this situation possible? Anything in life is possible, but to make moral decisions based on half-baked moral dilemmas is not logical or prudent.

The choice between the lesser of two evils is always a morally deficient option. I am not suggesting that we can make perfect decisions.

I am suggesting, however, that we should expand our options to protect the absolute principles that guide our lives. People can believe that their choices are limited to murder and lying. But the reality is that they would have to accept the fallacy of the ethical dilemma in which two options—and only two options—are available for the friend in the house. As we saw in the previous paragraph, the two options are artificially established to create the moral incongruence that ultimately rejects absolute principles. The final decision is presented as the choice between two equally reprehensible alternatives.

Let me share with you some of the house owner's alternatives to the previous ethical dilemma. First, he could choose not to open the door to the ax murderer. Second, if the murderer decides to break down the door, he could take his friend out the back door and run to a police station. Third, he could wait behind the door and hit the ax murdered with a bat as he enters, or he could call the police after the friend arrives and before the killer arrives at the house. The options are endless, but the ethical dilemma is not designed to find morally congruent solutions. It is designed to eliminate morally acceptable alternatives.

Faulty Examples

Boyd's logical fallacies are illustrated best by the four examples he used in his book to defend the thesis that God cannot know the future. His examples are not unique, but they are illustrative of open view reasoning. They reveal the open view's need to change the subject from a discussion about the nature of the future to a redefinition of the historical understanding of God's foreknowledge. Boyd's definition of the future is very simple: the future does not exist, and it cannot be known.[57] After all, there is more information about God's nature than there could possibly be about the unknowable and nonexistent future.

The first two examples from Boyd's book are hypothetical in nature. The third appears to be drawn from a real-life counseling experience, and the fourth is a feeble attempt to show how the open view defends God's omniscience without knowing the future.

---

[57] Boyd, 10.

First of all, Boyd describes his future purchase of a "tan-colored Acura." He advances the theory that if God knows the future, Boyd is not *truly free* to make the decision to purchase the car he really wants.[58] This example highlights the perceived contradiction between human freewill and God's foreknowledge.

The second example references the evil done by the twentieth-century dictator Adolf Hitler. This example pretends to illustrate the inevitable complicity that open view theologians see between God's foreknowledge and the evils he has allowed to come upon humanity.[59] This second contradiction is based on a similar presupposition—that is, a God with foreknowledge cannot be good in light of Hitler's evil. Allowing Hitler's grotesque existence would make the God of foreknowledge a tacit accomplice to Hitler's horrors. The implication is that the God of foreknowledge must either be the author of evil or find some redeeming value in evil to have created a man like Hitler.

The idea in open view theology also seems to be that the God of foreknowledge is in a constant and direct process of creating people. If God is still directly creating every individual, then we do not need the reproductive process. But God's specific command to Adam and Eve to "be fruitful and multiply" (Gen. 1:28 KJV) meant that God would not play an active role in the procreation process. Otherwise, the command would have been useless.

The third example describes the misfortunes of a woman identified by the name Suzanne.[60] This woman received what she understood was God's answer to her prayers regarding the man she wanted to marry. She later found out that God's answer to her prayers was deceitful. Her much anticipated marriage to the godly husband she had dreamed of turned into a nightmare. In fact, she married a philanderer who betrayed her within a few years of marriage. The final example has to do with a metaphor that suggests that God cannot be labeled as ignorant for not knowing something that does not exist.

These examples are not incidental to Boyd's theology. They are foundational to the practical application of his case. They go to the heart

---

[58] Boyd, 124.
[59] Ibid, 10; 98–99.
[60] Ibid, 104–106.

of the four basic assumptions proposed by open theists. These are (1) that we can maintain God's omniscience without the need to believe in the nonexistence of the human future, (2) that freewill negates the goodness of the God of foreknowledge, (3) that evil's existence is incompatible with a good God's foreknowledge, and (4) that as a practical matter, the God of foreknowledge must deceive humanity to control its decision-making process. Let's look at them in order.

Foreknowledge Is Incompatible With Freewill: The "Tan-Colored Acura" Fallacy

The "tan-colored Acura" example attempts to illustrate the incompatibility between human freewill and God's foreknowledge. Boyd stated,

> It is either true or false that I'll freely choose to buy a new tan-colored Acura on April 17, 2001. If God is omniscient, he must know all true statements as true and all false statements as false. Hence, he must know whether it's true or false that I will buy a tan-colored Acura in the future on this date.[61]

Boyd's statement is correct, as far as it goes. It is absolutely true that if God knows the future, then he knows everything exactly as it will occur. Obviously, if God knows the future, he must know whether Boyd is planning to buy a tan-colored Acura on April 17, 2001, or not. (Boyd wrote his book before 2001, and the references to that year are as if the event is still in the future.) Boyd added, "However, if you change your statement to say you *may* buy a tan-colored Acura on April 17, 2001, that statement is already true or false" [emphasis added].[62]

The reader cannot miss the following point. The argument appears to be that God may or may not know that Boyd could buy a tan-colored Acura on April 17, 2001, and that ambivalence makes the statement true or false. Of course, that statement is true or false. What else could it be? Boyd will either buy or not buy the tan-colored Acura on that day. But that's not the question that occupies us. The question is whether God knows in fact if it is true or false that Boyd will buy a tan-

---

[61] Boyd, 122–123.
[62] Ibid, 124.

colored Acura on that date. In other words, Boyd is saying that God cannot know the type of car Boyd will buy on that day. He only knows that Boyd could buy, or could not buy, a tan-colored Acura. I know that much about almost anything in the world. According to Boyd, this type of knowledge is a more accurate description of God's foreknowledge than if God knew for sure what Boyd would actually do on that day. In spite of the open view's claim to the contrary, this type of knowledge is not knowledge at all.

If I said that my son may or may not buy a car tomorrow, I have not said anything about my son's intentions or about tomorrow. Potential knowledge is a fantasy. There is no such thing. In order for knowledge to be real knowledge it must be true in fact. Boyd described God's knowledge of the future as a series of possibilities, which is basically the same as saying that God does not know anything about the future. Imagine if God had revealed the following to Daniel: There is the possibility that four or five or maybe six kingdoms will arise in the future that *could* determine the course of human history, but again there might not be because no one really knows what the future will bring. Now, let me ask you, what kind of knowledge is that? How many readers would believe that God had any actual knowledge regarding how many world kingdoms were yet to come?

Let me illustrate further. If you know the possibility that I may get up at 8:00 a.m., or at 9:00 a.m., or at noon, can it really be said that you actually know the time I will get up tomorrow? In reality, you don't have a clue. If God knows only the possibilities, then he knows that I could get up at any time between 8:00 a.m. and noon or not at all. You can call this suggestion many things, but knowledge is not one of them. If this is how the God of the open view knows the future, then he does not have the slightest idea at what time I will get up tomorrow either.

Boyd added that a "statement is true if it corresponds with reality."[63] The previous statement is a straitjacket definition of reality. Since, according to the open view, the future does not exist and cannot be known, logically, there is nothing about the future that corresponds to reality. The unavoidable conclusion is that any statement about the future can never be conclusively true because, in open theism's system,

---

[63] Boyd, 124.

the future does not correspond to reality. Boyd does not leave any room for discussion. Not only is he sure that the future does not exist even in the form of exhaustive information, he has claimed that nothing in the future corresponds to reality.

This definition complicates the openness problem. Boyd said that statements about the future do not correspond to reality "unless you *assume* the future already exists."[64] He does not define *reality*, but his statement suggests that reality is limited to verifiable historical facts. Or, said in other words, the only way the future corresponds to reality is if we assume that it is already historically verifiable. My contention here is *not* that the future exists as a concrete reality. My argument is that the future exists in God's mind in the form of exhaustive, noncausative information. However, if Boyd's statements were true, then he contradicts his own assertion that God had remarkable knowledge about the crucifixion. If God had remarkable knowledge about the crucifixion, then, this would also mean that God's knowledge about the crucifixion did not correspond to reality because it was not historically verifiable. Therefore, even in the case of the crucifixion, God's knowledge would be false because the prophecies did not conform to reality, according to Boyd's definition.

The problem for open theists is that, as far as I know, no one is arguing that the future "already exists" in the form of a human historical fact. If that was the case time travel would be possible and a DeLorean could take us back in time. The issue that concerns us here is whether God has advance exhaustive and non-causal information regarding the choices humans will make. The fact that God knows all statements as they really are, whether true or false, does not negate Boyd's ability to make a free choice regarding his desire to buy a tan-colored Acura on April 17, 2001.

Boyd's decision to buy a tan-colored Acura will not be made based on what God knows or does not know. His final decision will be made solely based on what he knows about his own desires and needs. He could lose his freedom only in two ways: if God forced him to purchase a different car than the one he desired, or if God forced him to purchase the tan-colored Acura after he had changed his mind regarding

---

[64] Boyd, 124.

his original intentions. Since biblical revelation affirms human freedom in the form of moral responsibility, it follows that God's knowledge cannot be determinative to Boyd's decision to buy, or not buy, this car.

God designed our decision-making mechanism so that he does not have, or need, to be the primary causal agent for our activity. He has provided people with enough information to allow them to make free decisions within their natures and circumstances. Even though people do not have exhaustive information, they are still responsible for their moral choices based on the available information they have at the decision point. By the way, I don't believe God cares one-bit what car anyone drives. God's only concern is with our ability to distinguish between good and evil. God did not lose one second of sleep when Adam was naming the animals in the garden. But he was greatly concerned when Adam decided to partake of the tree "of the knowledge of good and evil."

Boyd believes that if God knows with absolute certainty what he will do on April 17, 2001, then he loses the ability to make free choices about his own future. His fear of losing his freedom is based on the fallacy that God's knowledge is compulsive. God's knowledge is not, and cannot be, the determining factor in Boyd's decision, mostly because God's knowledge is not causative. This is true about all knowledge. No one is forced to do anything in his life based on someone else's information, and this is a verifiable fact. Open theists know things I do not know. I can affirm with certainty that I have never taken anything open theists know in consideration to make my own decisions. I do not know what they know. I do not care about what they know. As a matter of fact, when I read Boyd's book in 204, I had lived my entire life without making a single decision based anything open theists knew. Therefore, what they know cannot affect my decision-making process. We can apply this principle to God. The fact that God has advance knowledge of people's future decisions do not hinder them from freely making those decisions. Boyd remains free to act according to what he knows, unrestricted by what God knows.

Information possessed by a free moral agent does have the inherent ability to deny freedom of action to another free moral agent. For instance, I know for a fact that airplanes make transportation easier for people. But I am sure that not one single tribe in the Brazilian jungle has lost any sleep about the fact that they have never flown a plane. As a matter of fact, I am willing to bet that they have never made one single decision based on the fact that I can travel via airplanes, and they cannot. If God's knowledge of the future denies human freedom in the future, then, we should be able to conclude that God's perfect knowledge of the present eliminates human choice in the present. That's nonsense!

Let us return to Boyd's hypothetical example. Once Boyd makes the decision to purchase his tan-colored Acura, it cannot be said that God will be surprised by this decision. Boyd himself could not have known with certainty that he would be alive on April 17, 2001. Even if we grant that he could know his future with absolute certainty, this knowledge does not negate God's knowledge of the same future. God has not revealed how much he knows about Boyd's potential purchasing power. As such, there is no real basis to indict God's foreknowledge based on what a person does not know about his own future. The question is not, "What will Boyd do on April 17, 2001?" The real question is, "Will God be surprised by his decision?" I suggest that God already knows whether Boyd will change his mind.

As a general rule, I venture guess that people do not have the slightest idea about what God may know about anything he has chosen to keep secret. Actually, Boyd can only speculate that since he has not made a final decision regarding the kind of car he will buy on April 17, 2001, God cannot know what he is intending to do. However, if God knows anything about the future and chooses not to reveal this knowledge, then the open view is, at best, a wild speculation about what its proponents do not know about God. In *The God of the Possible,* Boyd stated,

> I deny that the statement "I will choose to buy a tan-colored Acura on April 17, 2001," is either true or false *(unless of course, God has indeed predestined this, or present causes render it certain).*[65] [Emphasis added]

Let me clearly state that the parenthetical statement makes the initial premise false. Let me explain. If God can predetermine Boyd's purchase of a car, then God has foreknowledge of that aspect of Boyd's future, which is precisely the opposite of what open theism stands for. If God

---

[65] Boyd, 124.

cannot have information regarding the future, then God cannot predestine Boyd's purchase of a tan-colored Acura, or any future human event, without predetermining every event leading to the purchase of that car and without violating freewill. After denying that the future exists, Boyd assures us that God can actually predestine the purchase of his car. Two questions arise—How does Boyd differentiate between predetermining and foreknowing the future? If God can predetermine Boyd's purchase of the car, doesn't that mean that this particular future "is there to be known"?

Boyd cannot categorically deny the veracity of his own statement because he does not know if the God of the open view in fact has predetermined the event. His escape hatch, "unless God has predestined the event," is a ridiculous statement for someone who dedicated an entire book to rejecting the proposition that the future exists. His suggestion is that the only future that God can know is the future he has predestined. This is exactly the same position of theological determinists. The obvious problem with this statement is that God's predestined future is always in relationship with humans (free moral agents), and open theism insists that future human decisions do not exist to be known because they have not been created and do not correspond to reality. If God can choose to predestine the purchase of Boyd's car, that would mean that God can predestine uncreated human events, which contradicts everything open theists stand for. Several additional observations are in order.

First, future human choices cannot be determined in the present to be absolutely true or false, and a statement cannot be true and false at the same time. The best we can say is that since we do not know what will happen tomorrow, we cannot ascertain the accuracy of any particular statement or action. A person's desire or a wish about what they intend to do in the future does not make the future certain for them one way or another. Boyd can always choose to buy a different car at the last minute or to not buy a car at all. Therefore, a person cannot know the truthfulness or falsehood of any statement regarding his own future. Future decisions and subsequent actions have too many variables to be predictable for people in the present.

Second, Boyd's statement is true only in that he cannot know the absolute truthfulness of any future event. People do not even have exhaustive information about the present, even when they are able to make the most meticulous plans. If information about the present is sketchy, at best, the logic of open theism must mean that we are not free even in the present time. God, on the other hand, has exhaustive information about the present, and it would not be a stretch to extrapolate that he has the same level of information about the future. The Bible is filled with prophecies that speak about God's knowledge of the future. The evidence points to God's foreknowledge and not away from it.

Third, Boyd's parenthetical statement opens a Pandora's box when he says that God cannot know the truthfulness of a statement "unless of course God has indeed predestined this, or present causes render it certain." This is precisely the classical view's point. Boyd rejects the classical view's hermeneutics that God can predestine everything because nothing in the future exists. And then he inserts the contradiction that God, indeed, might have chosen to predestine some things. Open theism cannot reconcile this contradiction. After rejecting the notion that the future may exist in the form of information, to suggest that God has the capacity to predestine future events in which people are involved is to introduce a logical impossibility. If this is the official position of openness theology, then open theism's central thesis that the future does not exist is rendered inoperative by its own internal arguments.

If the future does not exist to be known, it is impossible to say, as Boyd has done, that God is able to predestine his future purchase of a tan-colored Acura. It appears the open view's entire body of theology hinges on the possibility that God may have predestined only *some* things. If this is what its proponents want to promote, then they should not dismiss God's knowledge of the future outright as they have done. Foreknowledge is *advanced information of things to come,* not necessarily the preordination of them.

Taken together, Boyd's statements are irreconcilable contradictions that neutralize the most significant arguments within openness theology. On the one hand, he said that his statement regarding the purchase of the Acura is neither true nor false, but if we talk about possibilities, the statement is already true or false. Of course, it is possible that Boyd may or may not buy an Acura in 2001. We do not need God to know that. He also leaves open the possibility that God may have the power to preordain this particular event without revealing it to him, which means that God would know his decision before he makes it. The exception clause in the parentheses invalidates the initial premise. In other words, according to Boyd, God can predestine his purchase of the tan-colored Acura without telling him, negating his own argument that God's knowledge of such an event is impossible and would eliminate his freedom. This, by default, means that even within open theism, humanity's sense of freedom remains an illusion, and Boyd's statement is logically incongruent.

Since Boyd does not know if God predestined his purchase of the Acura, how can he say that the statement does not have a connection to a future reality or that he rejects the statement as either being true or false? If God has predestined Boyd's purchase of the Acura, then it would be absolutely true that Boyd will in fact purchase the Acura. However, how does Boyd square God's possible predestination of this particular event with his other statement that the future actions of future free agents do not exist and that not even God can know them? If it is possible for God to predestine particular events, then he has more information about the future than open theists are willing to admit.

It goes without saying that outside of his intent to buy a tan-colored Acura, Boyd cannot know anything else related to the events of April 17, 2001. He does not have access to any information about the future that could insulate him against the innumerable influences he has to overcome to accomplish his wishes. For example, the dealership could have had a fire that destroyed all the cars, or the owner could get shot on the way to the dealership, or Boyd could be forced to wait until a later day to buy his coveted car because of rain. In fact, there could be millions of these inconveniences. None of them are hindrances to his freedom in his decision-making process. However, any and all of these contingencies could alter his best-laid plans. The fact that he cannot account for all contingencies does not negate his freedom. On the contrary, having limited options confirms our freedom to make choices based on the level of information we have, not based on anything that anyone else may know, including God.

If Boyd changes his mind and buys a Chevy on April 17, 2001, that act proves his freedom, not the lack of it. He is free to change his mind, to deceive others, and even to try to deceive God. However, his free actions do not prove or disprove the extent to which God foreknows the event. Therefore, Boyd's final decision regarding the purchase does not contradict anything God knows. Nor does it interfere with anything he wants to do. Let me share a couple of concluding thoughts for this section.

First, Boyd will make his decision regarding the purchase of the Acura based on what he knows. He needs to know the vehicle's qualities, the cost, his taste, and his budget. Once he has analyzed the issues related to the purchase, he is ready to make the decision. The possibility that the dealership is planning to rip him off does not play a role in his decision-making process. Boyd's ignorance of the dealer's intent does not negate his freedom of choice. He can make his decision based only on what he knows, not on what he does not know.

Second, God's exhaustive knowledge of the present does not negate human freedom in the present. Conversely, God's exhaustive knowledge about the future is not a factor in a person's decision-making process because people never make decisions in the future. Knowledge possessed by another cannot be the determining factor in humanity's freedom. God is free to influence human choices by making information available to us through revelation, as he often does. Similarly, people can influence one another's decisions by sharing information.

For instance, let us say that you are about to purchase diamond stocks from a Nigerian prince who left a fortune to one of his heirs. Let's say that you are considering buying such stocks, but I know that this is a fraudulent scheme perpetrated on unsuspecting individuals. Finally, let us say that I show you how the scheme works. Would you buy the stocks, or would you not buy the stocks? If you do not buy the stocks, then the information I had regarding this scheme influenced your purchasing decision. However, the fact that I influenced your decision does not negate your freedom to buy or not to buy the stocks. People are influenced by new information all the time. When we read a book or a newspaper or listen to a speaker, we are receiving information that has the potential to influence us. Information always influences our decisions, but it would be ridiculous to suggest that lack of information takes away our freedom. At worst, lack of information takes away some of the options but never our freedom.

Freewill is God's gift to us, and it is only possible when God restrains his power and does not exercise external compulsion to make people act against their best interests. A free decision does not have to be a good decision. It only has to be made without coercion. The reality is that men and women are able to make free choices without divine interference, as demonstrated by Adam and Eve.

Foreknowledge As Incompatible With God's Goodness: The Hitler Fallacy

In the second hypothetical situation, Boyd utilizes the example of twentieth-century dictator Adolf Hitler to argue that God's foreknowledge is incompatible with his goodness. Boyd's argument is that God would not have created such a monster if he had known ahead of time what Hitler would do. This is the most careless of all the accusations Boyd made. He suggests that the God of foreknowledge must find redeeming value in evil.[66] He stated that, "if God is all good and thus always does what is best, and if God knew exactly what Hitler would do when he created him, we must conclude that God believed that allowing Hitler's massacre of the Jews (and many others) was preferable to his not allowing it."[67]

Boyd's implication is twofold: (1) the God of foreknowledge is in cahoots with evil to achieve his purposes, and (2) God found that *creating* Hitler was preferable to preventing his birth. This statement puts the open view in a precarious position. His former implication can be answered thus—the fact that God has knowledge of future events and persons does not prove causality or cooperation. It only means that God is painfully aware of humanity's capacity for evil. The latter implication can be answered this way—since God has not directly created anyone since Adam and Eve, he knew about Hitler, but he did not create him or want to prevent his birth.

The other problem for open theists is that if God does not have foreknowledge, he must be the most impotent deity ever conceived. Boyd cannot escape his own logic. First of all, Hitler's birth would have

---

[66] Boyd, 10; 97–101.
[67] Ibid, 98.

caught the God of open theism by surprise. Second, the God of open theism could not have known what Hitler was going to do in the present time until after Hitler finished his work. Please remember that Boyd has already argued that God cannot know uncreated future events until free agents have created them. Thus, the God of open theism could not do anything about Hitler's birth or even his actions. But this argues against open theism's tenet that God knows the present perfectly. If the God of foreknowledge had the obligation to prevent Hitler's birth, then the God of open theism had the obligation to give him a massive heart attack the very first time he spoke of the "Jewish solution." The logic works both ways.

Boyd appears to suggest that the God of foreknowledge is, by the very fact that he knows the future, complicit with the ravages of evil. A similar argument can be made against the God of the possible. Boyd has stated that the God of the possible "knows all possibilities."[68] Logically, the God of the possible anticipated the possibility of evil. The God of the possible also anticipated the kind of damage that evil people would bring upon the world, and yet, he did nothing to stop the procreation process to prevent a full expression of evil. This fact makes the God of the possible as negligent and as complicit with evil as the God of foreknowledge. If the God of the possible did not anticipate evil's appearance, he must have been shocked beyond belief when Adam and Eve rebelled against him. Can you imagine his shock when Cain killed Abel? The God of the possible must have watched in horror as people took a turn from bad to worse. Why didn't the God of open theism make every man and woman sterile to prevent future evil acts? Additionally, if the God of the possible anticipated Hitler's evil and did nothing about it, he is as guilty of evil as the God of foreknowledge.

The Hitler analogy has two additional problems. First, while God has the power to do anything he wants, generally speaking, God is not in the business of provoking the abortions of every potential sinner. Since everyone born is a sinner, we would have to make the same argument for God's intervention to prevent the birth of every potential petty thief that would be born. God has never been the primary active agent in the human procreation process. He designed men and women

---

[68] Boyd, 12.

with the built-in capacity to procreate. He then gave them the commandment to be fruitful and multiply, and people have multiplied. Therefore, Hitler's birth was a result of a natural process from within a fallen and sinful system.

The God of the open view has an even greater problem with Hitler because he knew the possibilities of Hitler's evil and stood still without taking action. Boyd believes that the God of foreknowledge should have taken action, but he gives a pass to the God of the possible, who could be as guilty of what he accuses the God of foreknowledge of not doing. The problem is that the God of the possible has also remained silent and uninvolved in Hitler's life for at least ten years.

Second, Hitler's example presents the God of open theism as an impotent God, even in the present time. According to Boyd, the God of foreknowledge should have done something to prevent Hitler's birth. However, why doesn't Boyd have the same expectation regarding the God of the open view's obligation to give Hitler a massive heart failure or a pulmonary embolism when he discovered Hitler's plans? If we accept Boyd's logic, the moment the God of open theism became aware that Hitler intended to incinerate six million people, he had to take action. The fact that the God of open theism did nothing to prevent the Holocaust is not an argument in favor of open theism. On the contrary, it makes open theism a shallow theology that can make accusations without offering real answers. The problem of evil cannot be resolved by saying that God just did not know what was going on, because even the God of open theism must have *known* what was going on.

The difference between the two perspectives is that the God of foreknowledge has a plan to bring a final and ultimate correction to evil, while the God of open theism is searching for a solution to the problem of evil as we speak. The God of open theism cannot prevent evil's drastic consequences as history moves recklessly toward chaos. In other words, the issue of evil cannot be brushed aside by making a broad accusation of complicity between the God of foreknowledge and evil. There are two ways that the God of foreknowledge could prevent Hitler's birth: (1) He would have had to interrupt the natural human procreation process for Hitler's mother by killing the unborn child, or (2) he would have had to make Hitler's mother unable to bear children. If the God of foreknowledge would have taken either option, he would have violated the woman's freewill. If God would have done as Boyd suggests, he would have destroyed the very purpose for which he created people with freewill.

The Hitler example is a particularly poor attempt to separate God from evil. Boyd's use of one of the most repulsive examples of fallen humanity to indict God's goodness does not do justice to God, and it does not speak well for open theists' methodology. The argument leads to the conclusion that only an immoral God who is in cahoots with evil would have allowed Hitler's birth. What stopped the God of open theism from giving Hitler a heart attack, a stroke, or a pulmonary embolism to kill him before he could do all the damage he did? After all, the defenders of this perspective claim that the God of the open view knows all the possibilities and is able to read a person's character with perfection. At some point, open theism's God should have known that Hitler had become a monster and should have disposed of him.

God's goodness, in open view theology, is predicated by the absence of foreknowledge. If this is true, then God's goodness must also be incompatible with his present knowledge. After all, evil is going on right now, and the God of open theism is allowing it to run wild on the countryside. If the God of open theism is as concerned with evil as open theologians claim, then he needs to take action right now to prevent all the evil that is going on at this very moment. The God of open theism should have been able to solve the Hitler issue easily and early. The moment that Hitler declared his intentions to rid the world of Jews, the God of open theism should have prepared the circumstances that would have allowed one of the many would-be assassins to succeed, and—voila—all the problems of the world would have been solved. Forgive my sarcasm, but Boyd's solution to the problem of evil solves nothing.

The bottom line is that Hitler's example is a red herring. If open theists can argue logically that God should not have created Hitler, then the same logic demands that God should not have created people at all. We know that other human beings committed other atrocities before Hitler was born. As a matter of fact, the God of open theism should have ended the human race after Cain killed Abel (Gen. 4). If the God of the open view had any doubts about humanity's capacity for evil, Abel's death should have dispelled them. We all know that it takes only one sin to disqualify people from a relationship with God. Therefore, God's *mistake* was not in creating Hitler. If we follow the open view's argument, God's *mistake* was in creating Adam and Eve. The logic of open theism cannot be allowed to stand.

While Hitler might be the epitome of human evil, he is nothing more than an extreme example of the human potential for evil when people live outside God's will. Using Hitler to indict God's foreknowledge is an attempt to arouse an emotional response from the readers, but it does not address the issue of God's foreknowledge. There is one thing that Hitler's example brings to the discussion: open theists mistakenly think they have a winning argument. We must conclude that if Hitler's creation is such a clear moral decision for open view theologians, then God's creation of Hitler was an error of gigantic proportion.

Apparently, the God of open theism does not understand the consequences of his own creative activity. Their charge appears to be that if God knew about Hitler ahead of time and he "unleashed"[69] this monster on humanity, then the God of foreknowledge is responsible for Hitler's atrocities. I consider this to be a very inflammatory accusation regarding God's character, especially when we consider that the God of open theism, who open theists claim knows all the possibilities, can be accused of the same *misjudgment*.

The open view's approach does not come close to solving the problem of evil. Its proponents' logic does not encourage trust in God. Rather, the open view creates the image of a God in a constant reactive mode to human sinful behavior. The openness God looks more like the gods described in Greek mythology than the God described in the Bible. While their intent is not to diminish God, the "the law of unintended consequences"[70] is unyielding. The law of unintended consequences means that people cannot always foresee the ultimate results of their choices because they cannot anticipate all the possible consequences of their decisions. It appears that the only principle that can be gathered from open theism is that an ignorant God can blame the devil for all

---

[69] Boyd, 10.
[70] Robert King Merton (July 5, 1910–February 23, 2003) is credited with coining the phrase.

human problems. The open view wants God to pass the buck regarding the issue of evil.

The logical consequences of accepting openness theology are disastrous for biblical preaching. How so? you may ask. It is virtually impossible to imagine how anyone can encourage people to trust in God while believing that God cannot even guarantee that the answer to the simplest of prayers will not have undesirable unintended consequences to the believer. How can a preacher who believes that God is not in control of the consequences of his own answered prayers encourage a congregation to trust God? Open theism does not offer any comfort regarding God's providence, especially when the God of the open view can know only possibilities.

I do not pretend to have the final answer to a debate that has raged from time immemorial. But the solution that open theism presents for the issue of evil is too simplistic. The only option they have to uphold God's goodness, in light of their expressed presuppositions, is to redefine God's relationship to time. They suggest that God's ignorance of humanity's future insulates God from responsibility for human sin. Not one open theist has discussed how God's perfect knowledge of the present absolves God of human evil in the present.

Open theists have not addressed how the God of the open view remains good in light of his knowledge of the present. How is the goodness of the God of open theism affected if he knows every possibility and those possibilities include present evil? In this sense, the God of open theism is as guilty of evil in the world as the God of foreknowledge, if that's the game we want to play. If this is true, then their argument against foreknowledge falls apart.

In open view theology, the God of foreknowledge cannot have good intentions if he created people he knew would end up in hell. Boyd has suggested that under these conditions, foreknowledge could not be one of God's attributes.[71] The God of the open view has the same problem because he knew of the possibility that people would end up in hell, and he still created them. As long as we are trying to reconcile the perceived contradiction between God's goodness and evil in the world, the problem will remain. The best definition of evil is *an inside the*

---

[71] Boyd, 11.

system corruption of the created order. The extent to which God is willing to go to correct that internal corruption in the system is evidence enough of his goodness. Open theists have met the problem of evil and have punted.

Boyd suggested that to believe in God's foreknowledge, one must also believe that God is responsible for Hitler's birth and behavior. He asks, "If God foreknew that Adolf Hitler would send six million Jews to their death, why did he go ahead and create him?"[72] The premise of the question is shocking. Boyd's implication is that God had a direct role in Hitler's *creation*. His question ignores a fundamental truth that should be common knowledge. God has not created anyone directly since Adam and Eve.

The biblical reference to God as the Creator of every person on earth is a figure of speech referring to the creation of human life. It is common knowledge that God created people with a built-in mechanism for procreation and reproduction. Is it possible for God to stop any particular person from being born? Technically, it is. However, God created a world in which humans were to be "fruitful and multiply" (Gen. 1:28). That is, God placed the responsibility for reproduction in people's reproductive systems—designed by God. Biblical revelation does not support the idea that God manages his creation by preventing people from procreating. The gift of procreation comes from God and is a natural process within the functioning of human design. Thus, God *has not* created anyone directly since the first couple. The best that can be said is that God has exercised sovereignty over creation, to include the birth of every child on earth.

The *autonomous* aspect of the human procreation process is absolutely essential to ensure both God's impartiality and human freewill. God created people with a built-in mechanism (the reproductive system) that made us *cocreators* with him. God does not need to perform a special act of creation to continue human life on earth. If God were directly involved in creating every individual, then it would be fair to say that God is responsible for choosing who will be born and who will not, and his command to be fruitful and multiply would be meaningless.

---

[72] Boyd, 10.

God would also be responsible for choosing each person's level of poverty and sickness, and in some cases, he would be responsible for a child's level of retardation or intelligence. What kind of a God is this? Whether God knows the future or just all the possibilities, if he is this involved in the procreation process, what was the purpose of the commandment to "be fruitful and multiply"? He could have simply arranged an assembly line at the garden of Eden and let it run ad infinitum. Clearly, he did not choose this method.

Every act of procreation is a man-made decision. God created humans with this gift, and we are free to exercise the gift within the limitations imposed on us by God's sovereignty. A pregnancy does not have to be a well-thought-out decision. Pregnancies are the natural result of people exercising the gift, regardless of how careless or well-planned they might be. It is astounding to me to find well-known theologians with such a naive perspective of God's order of things unless they are counting on the readers' ignorance to get their point across.

Therefore, to attribute Hitler's birth to God's "unleashing a mad dog on society"[73] is a gross misrepresentation of God's character and of his role in the procreation process. Hitler was a product of God's creation only in that he was born within the human race. But Hitler's character was the product of his ancestors, his environment, his historical biases, his personal prejudices, and so forth. Boyd omits the troubling socio-geopolitical questions that influence societies and make them susceptible to the governance of tyrants and despots. Nazi Germany was not created in Hitler's days. The conditions that produced Hitler had been lurking under the surface for quite some time. In reality, given the proper conditioning, any small-time despot could develop into a Hitler. During the Nuremberg trials, a Holocaust survivor said of a Nazi war criminal on trial, "But for an accident of nature, there go I."

Let me add two more statements. First, God was not blind when he gave reproductive freedom to humanity. He knew that procreation decisions would rest on the creature and that nature and nurture would play a role in people's character formation. Second, God fully knew that a deterioration of the human sinful condition could lead to men like

---

[73] Boyd, 10.

Hitler. He certainly knew that with the gift of procreation his involvement was not *needed* to create every person who would be born. Is God able to intervene at any time he so chooses? The answer is yes. But it appears that he decided to reduce his involvement in the human procreation process to a minimum to safeguard his impartial judgments and human moral freedom.

God reversed the barrenness of several women in the Bible to confirm their faithfulness, and he blessed them with children of their own, to ensure that his salvation plan would proceed according to his purpose. But even in those cases, God did not engage in a special creation process that resulted in the children. He simply reversed the condition that prevented their pregnancies—their barrenness. Procreation, then, took place within the normal process of conception. Jesus's birth, like Adam and Eve's creation, is unique.

Let me ask the question more provocatively. Is it really up to God to decide who is born, where they are born, and how they live their lives? I believe that God knows everyone who will be born, when, and where, but he has chosen to let the gift of procreation run its course as he designed it. There is no question that God took a huge *risk* in eternity past when he decided to create free-willed creatures, but he was fully aware of the risk and put in motion a plan to counter the inevitable human rush to rebellion.

Boyd's premise, as it relates to Hitler, that if God knows the future he cannot truly be good, misses one important point. Hitler is not the product of God's direct creative activity. God did not determine his social formation or his home environment. Thus, Boyd's question—"Why would a good God unleash such a monster on humanity?"—is wrongheaded and irresponsible.[74] It is surprising that Boyd would ask the question this way. Why would he suggest that God is somehow at fault for Hitler's crimes? In order to show that God is responsible for Hitler's crimes, Boyd must establish a cause-and-effect relationship between foreknowledge and causality. Open theists must be able to trace Hitler's behaviors to God. According to the open view, Hitler's injustices are enough evidence to prove that God could not have known that Hitler would turn into a monster. This is not a serious proposal. If

---

[74] Boyd, 10.

anything, Hitler's evil only proves that God created people with moral freedom.

The debate about evil is, in reality, more about God's goodness than it is about God's foreknowledge. My contention is that God's goodness is not contingent on his foreknowledge even if both attributes define God's nature and character. Additionally, there is not an inherent correlation between God's foreknowledge and evil. God's foreknowledge means God has advance, exhaustive and non-causal information about future human choices and actions. Evil is a distortion introduced into God's created order by Satan and into the world by people (Rom. 5:12). God did not create or introduce sin into the universe. Sin is a violation of God's original purpose, and God's goodness is not in jeopardy as a result because he is distinct from his creation.

Foreknowledge is an attribute inherent in God's divine character, and it cannot have a negative relationship to his goodness. We can take the previous logic and extend it to other divine attributes. For example, since God is all-powerful, he can prevent hurricanes, earthquakes, and tornadoes from causing so much death and devastation. The argument can be made that God's goodness is compromised by his failure to prevent natural disasters. However, since we are playing the blame game, the God of open theism would have the same problems. If open theists want to make the argument that God does not have foreknowledge, they should focus on that without muddying the waters with a debate about God's goodness. All of God's attributes are complementary to one another, but they are not contingent on one another. In other words, none of God's attributes exists as a precondition for another attribute. All of God's attributes exist in God at the same time as part of his nature. Open theism's biggest problem, in utilizing evil as a supportive argument against foreknowledge, is that any of God's attributes can be used to argue against his goodness.

There is another issue that Boyd does not discuss in *The God of the Possible*. He does not provide a definition or an interpretation of evil. If evil is a measurable thing or an entity, then it must have been created by God. This fact should be evident enough because it exists within the created order. However, if evil is the rejection of God's goodness by the creature, then evil can exist without being created by

God. Paul wrote that sin "entered the world through one man" (Rom. 5:12). A correct interpretation of Paul's words leads to the conclusion that God did not create evil. Sin can be properly called a distortion introduced into the system by people acting on their free moral choices to reject God's goodness. Therefore, evil could not have been created by God, again, because evil is the rejection of God's goodness, not a consequence of it. Ravi Zacharias describes sin as "saying no in the face of God."[75] God did not create the distortion because everything he created was good (Gen. 1).

What can we say about Satan? Satan is the impersonation of evil. He is the maximum representation of the absolute absence of God's goodness. Allow me an illustration from the physical world.

Zero degrees Kelvin is the absolute absence of heat. It is equivalent to –459 degrees Fahrenheit. While heat is a measurable entity, cold is not. Heat is a created thing, but cold is not. Cold is the absence of heat. While we can experience both and speak of both as existing, one is the absence of the other. In a similar manner, evil is the absence of good. Satan's evil, therefore, represents the absolute absence of goodness. The devil cannot do anything but be evil. He is evil for evil's sake, and his evil is the distortion he introduced into creation when he rebelled against God by demanding and expecting worship. Isaiah describes Satan's attitude thus: "I will ascend above the tops of the cloud; I will make myself like the Most High" (Is. 14:14). Satan desired worship, but only the Creator is worthy of worship. It was this attitude that arose from the creature that introduced sin into the universe.

The skeptic could say that since God created Lucifer and since Lucifer turned evil with his pride and rebellion, it follows that God created evil. This conclusion is the classical "guilt by association" accusation. We could make this connection only if we assume that the premise is true that in creating Lucifer, God was intentionally introducing evil into the world to create havoc. The opposite is true. God was motivated by love, which found expression in a good creation. While God foreknew the emergence of evil, the resulting evil was the inevitable consequences that made the knowledge of good possible.

---

[75] Ravi Zacharias. http://delightinggrace.wordpress.com/2012/08/23/ravi-zacharias-on-sin/ (Accessed November 2012).

I can it in another way. When God created light, he did not create darkness—he revealed darkness so that we could appreciate the light. While some may say that this is a distinction without a difference, the fact remains that God was not the active agent that produced darkness or evil. God is light and good, and he was willing to tolerate evil in order to share his goodness with humanity. Paul suggested as much in Romans 9:22–24.

> What if God, choosing to show his wrath and make his power known, bore with great patience the objects of his wrath—prepared for destruction? What if he did this to make the riches of his glory known to the objects of his mercy, whom he prepared in advance for glory—even us, whom he also called, not only from the Jews but also from the Gentiles?

The apostle suggested that God chose to patiently tolerate human rebellion in order to make his goodness known to those who would choose to love him. Paul understood that God has no direct or indirect connection with the absence of good. God chose not to take an active role in preventing the manifestation of evil in order to show his goodness. The absence of goodness revealed the contrast that made humanity's desire for good possible. As the apostle states, "He bore with patience the objects of his wrath" (Rom. 9:22). This divine decision is essential so that the objects of mercy could distinguish goodness from evil. Without the presence of evil, the distinction cannot be made.

I am proposing that God foresaw evil's appearance and made a plan to counter its consequences but that he did not purposed (decree) evil into existence. The Bible is specific in stating that everything God created was good. This could only mean that evil was not an aspect of God's creation. God cannot be accused of being complicit with it because he exists outside the realm in which the "violation of purpose" emerged. God's goodness is an intrinsic value to God's character and has been since before creation. We can infer at least three conclusions. First, evil, as the absence of good, is not an integral part of God's nature. Second, evil is directly connected to the free actions taken by the creatures after and within creation. And finally, evil cannot tarnish God's nature or character because it is contained within creation while God exists outside and independently of it.

Applicability of the Open View: Suzanne's Fallacy

In the movie *Bruce Almighty,* the main character, played by comedian Jim Carrey, received some of God's powers for a short period of time to resolve all the world's problems, as the main character desired.[76] God, played by actor Morgan Freeman, gave Bruce the opportunity to fix the problems in his little world in Buffalo, New York. In one scene, Bruce had grown tired of people's prayers, and in a moment of frustration, he answered all of the prayers with a yes. That day, every person who played the lottery and prayed to win it, won (but each received only pennies), a woman lost forty pounds on the Krispy Kreme diet, and other miraculous answers to prayers were granted.

There was one problem—Bruce had no idea how his *yes* answer to all the prayers would affect the world around him. Of course, we are talking about a movie in which the character that played God did not understand that an answer to prayer will have consequences beyond the answer itself. However, open theism has actually given this movie plot a theological rationale. The God of open theism is like Bruce Almighty—he does not know how his actions affect people beyond the simple answer to prayers. This is the case with Suzanne. Let us examine this example from Boyd's book.

Of the four examples in Boyd's book, this is the saddest. I will treat Suzanne's case as a real-life story and not as a hypothetical illustration, although some of the elements in the story appear to be made up for the sake of the illustration.[77] Her experience is intended to show the practical applicability of the open view in everyday life. Boyd described Suzanne's story as if he had personally counseled her. The suggestion was that Suzanne and her story are real. The discussion here is not intended as a personal indictment on Suzanne in any way. This section should not be interpreted as a reflection on her personal circumstances. Rather, the intent is to analyze open view theology as explained through her example. It is my prayer that God has granted her peace of mind and provided her with comfort. However, we need to

---

[76] *Bruce Almighty*. Spyglass Entertainment, Universal Studios, 2003.
[77] Boyd, 103–106.

make an honest evaluation of her situation as Boyd described it in *The God of the Possible.*[78]

The following is a brief summary of Suzanne's case. Boyd described her as a godly woman committed to Taiwan as her mission field. She wanted to marry a young man who shared her missionary vision. Suzanne met such a man in Bible school and dated him for three years. After "a number of *coincidences*," as Boyd called them,[79] Suzanne married the man of her dreams. They prayed together, went to church together, and fasted together as they sought God's guidance regarding their desire to marry. Finally, God answered their prayers, we are told, and they were married. Suzanne and her new husband went to missionary school, and within two years, she discovered that the husband God had sent her was cheating on her.

Boyd used Suzanne's story to illustrate how God could not have known ahead of time that Suzanne's husband would cheat on her. If God had had prior knowledge of Suzanne's husband's infidelity, Boyd told us, then God intentionally withheld essential information that led her into an unhappy relationship. Suzanne concluded, and Boyd agreed, that God deceived her by answering a prayer that he knew would result in more harm than good.

Boyd's implication is that if God knew Suzanne's future, he either deceived her or intentionally brought misery into her life. I do not agree that these are the only options. For example, God could have been leading Suzanne in a different direction from the beginning, but she fell in love with her future husband and might have lost sight of God's real purpose for her life. She might have seen and ignored signs that the love of her life had a questionable character. Suzanne's husband could have realized that he was confused about his calling, or worse yet, Suzanne was confused about hers. The possibilities are endless. However, Boyd implies that the God of open theism is not guilty of Suzanne's fate because he did not know her husband's character. After all, what could the God of the possible do under those circumstances? The openness God had no idea that Suzanne's husband would turn into an adulterer.

---

[78] Boyd, 103-106.
[79] Ibid, 106.

I do not know about you but trusting the God of the possible is not easy, especially if he cannot make a simple character judgment. Boyd sees God's inability to warn Suzanne regarding her husband's character flaw as evidence that open theism has a more positive application for life. This means that open theism does not have to make excuses for God. Its proponents' assumption must be that since the God of open theism functions within limited cognitive parameters, he is innocent of Suzanne's predicament. After all, no one is accountable for something he knows nothing about.

The open view's practical application can be summarized as follows. Suzanne cannot blame God for her husband's failings because God did not know the man very well. She cannot blame God for his inability to give her sound advice because God did not know how her husband was going to respond. The God of the open view was helpless because he had no way to ascertain Suzanne's husband's upcoming unfaithfulness. Boyd's argument is that God's advice to Suzanne was based on his limited knowledge when he answered her prayers. God had good intentions, but they were based on unreliable information (the God of open theism simply did not know what her husband would do). Additionally, God's knowledge did not include any future activity that Suzanne's husband would engage in, and as such, God is not responsible for Suzanne's misery. The God of the open view simply had no way to protect Suzanne.

I do not know Suzanne, and I have no reasons to doubt her story as she experienced it. However, I am skeptical that her experience fits so nicely into open theism's paradigm. We do not know anything about her husband. We do not know if he had intimacy issues with Suzanne. We do not know if he was a scoundrel from the very beginning. If that was the case, even the God of open theism should have known about this man's character flaw. We are led to believe that Suzanne did not play any role in her husband's unfaithfulness, that she was the perfect Christian wife when tragedy befell her. While Suzanne may not have been able to discern her husband's character, the God of open theism should not have fallen prey for the same scheme.

According to Boyd, the God of foreknowledge did not provide sound and timely warnings that could have prevented Suzanne from marrying a cheating husband. Boyd takes the position that since

Suzanne was the perfect wife and her husband turned into the devil incarnate overnight, the God of the open view could do nothing to help her. The God of the open view must have been shocked out of his mind when he found out that Suzanne's husband cheated on her after he had answered her prayers in the affirmative. As a matter of fact, if it was up to Boyd, if God has foreknowledge, he owes Suzanne an apology for answering a prayer that turned into a curse. I am curious as to how the God of openness would have dealt with Suzanne's prayer. However, since the God of open theology does not have foreknowledge, he should not have recommended that Suzanne marry a man who God himself hardly knew. If the God of open theism knows people's characters perfectly, then he should not have recommended that Suzanne marry this particular man.

Apparently, Suzanne feels that the only possible solution to her dilemma—that God had answered her prayers that turned into a curse— was to accept God's ignorance of her future. I believe this option leaves Suzanne with a false hope. Since Boyd is illustrating God's lack of foreknowledge through Suzanne's example, that must mean that the God of open theism was unable to give Suzanne a clear picture of her husband's character. The alternative that the God of open theism was ignorant of Suzanne's husband's character is not a good defense of the system. This is especially true in light of the discussion on Peter's denials, as we will discuss later. In Peter's case, Boyd argues that God could predict Peter's three denials solely based on his perfect knowledge of Peter's character. I find it curious that God could predict Peter's denials based on the disciple's character, but he could not do the same for Suzanne. If the God of openness knows the whole of reality perfectly, then he must have known Suzanne's husband's character for a long time. However, if the God of openness can be so easily deceived, then I will take my chances with the God of foreknowledge.

Boyd left out a number of possible issues present in every failed relationship that could have assisted the reader to reach a more informed conclusion. For example, is it possible that Suzanne neglected her husband while in missionary school? Do we know if the husband had asked her to be more attentive? Could it be that they had communication problems? Is it possible that their finances were not in proper order? Maybe the husband was simply an idiot. But if this was the case, then even the God of the open view should have been able to warn her based on the man's explicit idiocy.

I am not suggesting that Boyd and Suzanne manufactured a conspiracy to deceive the readers. I am suggesting, however, that every relationship dispute has at least two sides, and I have not heard the husband's side so that I can make a proper evaluation of this case. Suzanne's case, as presented, is truncated and paints a distorted view of how most marriages work. It also misrepresents God's role in Suzanne's life. If counselors could not discern marital patterns, then marriage counseling would be all but impossible. Counseling professionals know that one-sided stories never provide an accurate picture for effective counseling. Additionally, one-sided counseling is patently unjust to the absent partner. How can Boyd explain that the God of open theism was not able to make a simple guess regarding Suzanne's husband's character?

Unfortunately for the open view, Suzanne's case does not shed any light on the foreknowledge debate. Her case cannot be properly evaluated to reach any solid conclusions regarding God's involvement in her life. I am not challenging Boyd's truthfulness, but when the implications are this far reaching, doubt is the better part of wisdom. Boyd should have presented a more comprehensive case history that included Suzanne's husband's side of the story, or he should have used a different story to better illustrate his point here. Boyd wanted to use this example to show that God's foreknowledge was not a positive asset when answering Suzanne's prayers. However, unless Boyd presents specific details of their relationship, such as her motives and her general impressions during the relationship, all Boyd is doing is slandering God's foreknowledge through the use of anecdotes.

Boyd goes on to say that "Suzanne could not fathom how the Lord could respond to her lifelong prayers by setting her up with a man he *knew* would do this to her and her child."[80] I do not know if these are Suzanne's exact words or if Boyd implied the meaning of the sentence from the information he gathered from Suzanne's answers and statements. The caution flag goes up here because the quote sounds way too much like Boyd's own theological perspective to be the perspective

---

[80] Boyd, 105.

of a former missionary school candidate who just experienced a painful betrayal and divorce. If she made the statement, she certainly sounded like she had already been indoctrinated in open view theology. If she had, then Boyd's use of her example is more deceptive than it appears on the surface.

There are two additional concerns with Suzanne's example. If the God of open theism answered Suzanne's prayers to marry her husband in the affirmative, at least one of two things must be true: The God of open theism does not understand how the law of unintended consequences operates, or Suzanne's husband deceived the God of the open view. In either case, this event does not paint a pretty picture about the character of the openness God. The chain of events that followed Suzanne's wedding made God completely unreliable when answering prayers—either that, or he is incapable of making the simplest of character evaluations.

After three and a half years of dating and two years of marriage, Suzanne was not able to notice a single trait in this man's character that could have given her doubts. It is even harder to believe that the God of open theism could make the same misjudgments as Suzanne, even though he had exhaustive information about the man's character. Boyd cannot be suggesting that Suzanne's husband was the perfect man before the wedding and turned into a philanderer after it without any warnings at all. This would be comical if it wasn't so tragic.

Let us assume, for Suzanne's sake, that she did not notice anything in her husband's character that would give her some doubts. However, to say that the God of the open view missed all the possible indicators that pointed to the man's deteriorating character is impossible to justify. Even the God of open theism, who knows all possibilities, could not have missed all of them. The God of the open view should have been able to make a better guess regarding this man's character.

It gets worse. Boyd expects his readers to accept the proposition that the God of the open view was honest when he answered Suzanne's prayers even though he did not take into account the possible consequences. Either Suzanne was blinded by her husband's charm and her love for him, as happens very often, or the God of the open view does not have a clue about human relationships and people's characters.

While Suzanne could have been blinded by her love, we should not accept the proposition that the God of the open view could have been so easily fooled. Otherwise, we have to conclude that Suzanne's husband was such a good con man that even the God of open theism fell for his deception. This is not a pretty sight.

To chalk up this error in judgment to the theory that God does not know the future is, at best, reckless. The premise that the God of open theism can answer prayers without knowing their possible consequences is asinine. The idea that Suzanne is now free to continue trusting God because, after all, he tried his best, is not credible. I would rather make my own decisions without prayers than to rely on the God of the open view who has no clue why he is answering prayers.

When the God of the open view told Suzanne that he approved of her marriage to her husband, it was based, I assume, on flawed information—*He did not know any better*. This error was nobody's fault. Suzanne trusted God. God answered her prayers honestly but in ignorance. Suzanne's husband deceived her and conned God. The God of open theism was impotent to help her because he did not have enough information to make an educated guess. This is not possible.

The God of open theism's *approval* of Suzanne's marriage looks like a miscalculation of gigantic proportions. Suzanne was blinded by her love. Fine. That happens. Her counselors did not see any problems with her relationship to this man. Okay. Sometimes we miss some of the signs. However, to insist that the God of open theism missed the whole affair is simply not credible. If the God of the open view knows everything there is to know, how do open view theologians explain his inability to accurately discern this man's character before the wedding?

If God does not know the future and is prone to make such misjudgments in the present, why does he even get involved in answering prayers at all? If the God of open theism is not able to judge human character, then it follows that none of us should trust him. We can never know if the God of open theism's advice is sound and wise or if it comes from ignorance, as it did with Suzanne. Please understand— this is the same God that Boyd tells us could predict Peter's denials, a future event, solely based on the disciple's character.

The practical application of the open view does not provide as much comfort as open theists claim. It only makes our present condition even more miserable because we cannot even hope that the God of open theism can answer our prayers with any assurance that they will come through, or that if they come through, the unintended consequences would not harm us. Why would anyone pray to the God of the open view? How can the God of open theism promise that "all things work together for good" (Rom. 8:28) if He has no clue what those things are or how they will work together?

Monkey Business

Boyd stated that God's "lack of definite foreknowledge of future actions limits him no more than does the fact that, say, he does not know that there is a monkey sitting next to me right now. As a matter of fact, there is no monkey sitting next to me, so it's hardly ascribing ignorance to God to insist that he does not know one is there."[81]

The previous analogy has several problems of logic we need to address. First, if we can see that a monkey is not sitting next to us, then no one should expect that God would be able to see a monkey. Second, the monkey analogy is a reference to a physical, visible element that can be easily witnessed by anyone within eyesight of the event. Third, the analogy breaks down further because the nature of the future is an abstract concept without a physical point of reference. We cannot equate the concreteness of a physical object—the monkey, in this case—with the abstractness of nonphysical information.

Let us redraw the analogy. Let us say that a blind man has a monkey sitting next to him. Clearly, the blind man would not be able to see that there is a monkey sitting next to him. If God is like the blind man and he cannot see the monkey either, then, God and the blind man have the same problem. We are blinded to the future, and open view theologians argue that God is as blind to it as we are. So, if God cannot see the monkey sitting next to the blind man, then, the God of open

---

[81] Boyd, 16.

theism has no business guessing anything about monkeys sitting next to blind men.

However, the blind man's inability to see the monkey cannot be the standard by which we evaluate the reality around him. His blindness renders him incapable of judging with accuracy whether a monkey is sitting next to him. We can agree that people are blind to the future. Thus, people's blindness to the future cannot be the yardstick we use to evaluate God's capacity to have advanced information about the future. Humanity does not have access to God's eternal perspective. As a result, they are incapable of seeing that which has been hidden from them in eternity. The future is hidden from us in a similar manner that the monkey is hidden from the blind man. Our blindness of the future, like the blind man's blindness to see the monkey, is not evidence that God cannot see either.

The statement that "one is not ascribing ignorance to God by insisting that he doesn't foreknow future free actions if indeed free actions do not exist to be known until free agents create them" is an ingenious defense against the accusation that open view theologians have redefined the basic definition of God's knowledge.[82] If open theists could actually prove that God's knowledge is limited to what free moral agents create, as Boyd has stated, then they would have reduced God's capacity to know to an inferior level to humanity. At least people can create their own futures, but God can only know what people create. What a pitiful state of affairs.

If Boyd's statement is true, then humans play a determinative role in God's ability to know. This is an asinine assertion mainly because God had knowledge before the creation of people. Fortunately, divine revelation is the only known method we have to ascertain whether God knows something. McCabe argued that God learns about the future as it unfolds.[83] McCabe believed that the Bible teaches a nescient doctrine of God. Our contention here is that the Bible says nothing about a nescient doctrine of God. The safe thing to assume, of

---

[82] Boyd, 17.

[83] Lorenzo McCabe, *Divine Nescient of Future Contingencies a Necessity* (New York: Phillips and Hunt, 1882), 27.

course, is that God has exhaustive knowledge about the universe he created, to include the future.

Boyd's example does not shed any light regarding God's cognitive limitations. He does not even make an attempt to address God's instantaneous knowledge as it relates to time. He simply implies that God's existence outside of time is irrelevant to his ability to know. If one day is like a thousand years and a thousand years like one day for God, then whatever limitations God may or may not have regarding his knowledge are not determined by time (2 Pet. 3:8). God's scope of knowledge is so vast that the apostle Peter could only describe it in eternal terms.

Since open view theologians have concluded that the future does not exist and cannot be known, their definition of the future is a fallacy. This is like the blind man who swears that a monkey is not sitting next to him because he cannot see him. And armed with their blindness of the future, they project their blindness onto God.

Recapping

Boyd suggested at least three basic principles in his book. First, if God knows the future, people are not free to make decisions without external compulsion. The simple answer to this claim is that as long as the God of foreknowledge is not the causal agent for the human decision-making process, his knowledge is not a *de facto* infringement on human freewill. The issue is not whether we can change our minds; the real issue is whether God is surprised when we do. Open theists would like us to believe that God is in a constant reaction mode to our creativity. However, since God's knowledge is not a violation of humanity's freewill, the argument falls on account of its own weight.

Second, if God knows the future, he is responsible for evil. Boyd used Hitler's example to argue this point. The logic appears to be unassailable. It goes like this:

(a) God created every person that has been born.

(b) Hitler was a person.

(c) Hitler was evil.

(d) God is responsible for Hitler's birth

(e) God is responsible for Hitler's evil.

The logical progression fails on the first premise. Since Adam and Eve, God has not directly created anyone. People are the result of the God-given procreation mechanism. Hitler was God's creation only in that he was born within the human race. If God had to stop Hitler's birth because he would turn into a monster, then God should not have created people at all. Hitler is but one example of the countless evil people who have roamed the earth. God's motives for creation, or his understanding of evil, cannot be evaluated through Hitler's immoral life.

Finally, Boyd suggested that the character of the God of open theism is more compatible with human experience. I disagree. On the one hand, Boyd has argued that the God of open theism could predict Peter's denials solely based on his knowledge of Peter's character. On the other hand, Boyd assured us that the God of open theism was impotent to use Suzanne's husband's character as the basis to protect her. When we consider the God of open theism's involvement in Suzanne's case, he is an inept and confused deity answering prayers he cannot support.

The God of open theism is a superhuman who has a great deal of power, but like us, he does not know how to achieve his objectives in human affairs without controlling and manipulating people. He also appears to be callous for answering prayers without considering their consequences. Boyd finds comfort in God's ignorance, but most people would be frightened by such a prospect. It is not theologically sound to teach that God answers prayers and then leaves people to fend for themselves against the inevitable unintended consequences.

After considering these four examples, the God of open theism appears to be tyrannical, powerless, blind, and untrustworthy. How can anyone trust a God who cannot even answer prayers honestly? Thanks, but no thanks. As for me, I will continue to pray to the God of foreknowledge who knows and holds my future.

The revelation of Jesus Christ, which God gave him to show his servants what must soon take place. He made it known by sending his angel to his servant John, who testifies to everything he saw—that is, the word of God and the testimony of Jesus Christ.

—Revelation 1:1–2

Chapter THREE
Prophecy and the Open View

One of baseball's great players, and an amateur philosopher, Yogi Berra, once said that "predicting things is very hard, especially the future." While Berra's statement was not intended to be a theological principle, it highlights the open view's prophetic problem. The fact is that knowing the future is an exclusive divine prerogative. God considers human predictions as demonic for they are the result of false teaching and man-made gods and idols (Is. 46:10). God has claimed exclusive rights to reveal the future.

Open theism has many problems, but none is greater than prophecy. If open theism is true, then God has no business claiming that he can reveal the future. In this chapter, we will address the prophetic problem for open theism, including a discussion on Jesus's prediction of Peter's denial, which has been offered as proof that God does not need to know the future to make predictions.

Simply put, prophecy is not possible without foreknowledge. Open theism has adopted Lorenzo McCabe's "nescience" principle as a

101

critical aspect of its theology—it simply means that God does not know. McCabe argued that God was fighting evil without knowing ahead of time the next place the evil would make its entrance.[84] In discussing this principle, Jowers stated that the "affirmation of divine ignorance implies that God's expectations may at times be mistaken. If this is so, then God's prophesying that an event will occur in Scripture constitutes no guarantee of the event's actual occurrence."[85] In Jowers's view of the nescience principle, God cannot even guarantee that his prophecies will be fulfilled in fact. Not only that, but the teaching about God's nescience makes biblical inerrancy an unsustainable doctrine. Jesus said, referring to Scripture, "Your Word is truth" (John 17:17), but open theists say, *Maybe.*

Jesus also said, "Scripture cannot be broken" (John 10:35 KJV), but open theists suggest that just because God has revealed something does not mean that it will come to pass, or that he was serious about it. Pinnock stated as much when he said, "We may fail to admit it, but prophecies often go unfulfilled."[86] Pinnock's statement suggested that biblical revelation is fallible and, thus, unreliable. This is a clear attack on the biblical doctrine of inerrancy and the veracity of God's character, even if Pinnock was not aware of the implications of his words. In fairness to Pinnock, he later backpedaled from this assertion when confronted by his denomination for his possible heresy.

Basinger, another proponent of openness theology, when explaining God's knowledge, flatly stated, "We maintain, further, that God possesses only what has come to be called 'present knowledge.'"[87] Open view theologians also "believe that God can never know with certainty what will happen in any context involving freedom of choice."[88] The only possible conclusion, based on open theism, is that God can never predict anything in the future that includes human activity. Therefore, prophecy is a figment of the biblical writers' imagination. Open theism has effectively turned God into a delusional

---

[84] McCabe, 61.

[85] Dennis W. Jowers, "Open Theism: Its Nature, History, and Limitations" *WRS Journal* (Feb. 2005): 1–9.

[86] Pinnock, *Most Moved Mover*, 51.

[87] David Basinger, *The Openness of God* (Downers Grove, IL: InterVarsity Press, 1994), 163.

[88] Boyd, 163.

liar because he has claimed that he "makes the future known" (Is. 46:10). Clearly, if the future cannot be known, then it cannot be revealed. In the same passage quoted earlier, God declares that the difference between him and idols is precisely his ability make the future known.

If God cannot make the future known, as the prophet Isaiah has revealed, then there is no difference between God and idols. The prophetic issue is a compelling argument to reject openness theology's present-knowledge proposition. On the one hand, open view theologians have told us that open theism is not about God's knowledge. They insist that they are defining the nature of the future.[89] On the other hand, Basinger, Pinnock, and Jowers have stated that God's knowledge must be reinterpreted to limit its scope to the present.

Openness theologians have created a Pandora's box for themselves. For instance, Boyd makes two statements that, taken together, are inherently and irrevocably contradictory. First, he tells us that "the future does not exist and cannot be known."[90] And then he adds that "God can predestine and foreknow *whatever he wants to* about the future."[91] Boyd's statement that God can predestine anything he wants could be an attempt to walk-back the more radical pronouncement made by other proponents of open theism that deny God's ability to know anything about the future. Boyd's contradiction was a feeble attempt to resolve the complications that the nescient doctrine brings into the openness debate. Boyd's solution is in the *Thank you for trying* category.

If Boyd's first statement is true, then nothing about people's future can be revealed because it does not exist to be revealed. This would render biblical prophecy meaningless. If the second statement is true, then God can predict at least some aspects of the nonexistent future. The problem should be obvious. There is no logical way to reconcile these two statements. Either, the future does not exist, and God cannot know it (or reveal it), or God can partly know the future and, thus, the future exists, even if God only has partial knowledge of it. If God partly knows the future, as Boyd has affirmed, at the very

---

[89] Boyd, 16.
[90] Ibid.
[91] Ibid, 31.

minimum, there must be an abstract conceptualization of the future. Additionally, the partly settled future concept suggests that God's knowledge, of a potentially knowable future, is not exhaustive. This proposition turns God's perfection on its head. Open theists may not see the contradiction, but until their contradiction and Basinger's present-knowledge theory are properly clarified with sound biblical hermeneutics, their theological system must be rejected.

Answering the Contradiction

While most open theists accept the nescient principle, Boyd makes an attempt to sidestep the implications of both Jowers's nescient principle and Basinger's present-knowledge principle. Let us take a look at Boyd's attempt to reconcile the contradiction.

Boyd suggested that the inherent contradiction within open theism can be resolved with the concept he calls the "partly settled future." He anticipated the objection to the partly settled future concept with the following question: "How can you claim that the future is *partly* open and *partly* settled?"[92] He answers his question with a defensive observation. "Initially [the partly settled/partly open dichotomy] strikes many people as contradictory."[93] The reason this concept strikes people as contradictory is because it is. The issue is not whether the two statements taken together are contradictory. That is painfully obvious enough. The real question is, how can a perfect God have *partial* knowledge of anything? Boyd does not even attempt to answer how the partly settled future concept affects God's perfection or his statement that the future does not exist to be known.

In spite of the confidence that Boyd pretends to have on the partly settle future concept, he moves rather quickly away from his contradictory principle. He spends most of his time explaining how people experience the future. He states, "*We* assume the future is partly open and partly settled with every decision *we* make" (emphasis added).[94] While it is true that we make plans for future activities based on known information, there is not a human alive who knows with

---

[92] Boyd, 144.
[93] Ibid.
[94] Ibid.

absolute certainty that his plans for the future will come to pass exactly as he has planned them. We have to point out that human assumptions about the future do not settle any part of it. A partly settled future, from the human perspective, is at best a desire expressed in a decision and at worst wishful thinking. But how can any part of the future be settled in a person's mind? It cannot be. There is one simple reason people cannot settle anything in the future—they do not live there.

The argument from human experience that all our decisions are based on a partly settled and partly open future is logically deficient and experientially false. Boyd describes the human decision-making process in the following way. First, a person "can't deliberate between options unless (a) most of the future is predictable and not up to me to decide, and (b) the matter of deliberation *is* genuinely 'open' and 'up to me' to resolve."[95] The reader should note that these suggestions have nothing to do with God or the future. They are both related to a person's present knowledge and state of mind. The ability to debate future options to make them congruent, or resolve them, has no direct correlation to God's knowledge.

Several additional observations are in order. Boyd's discussion regarding the congruency between the partly settled and partly open future concepts misses the point. He illustrated his principle through human experience. However, we cannot extrapolate human experience to equate it with God. The pertinent issue before us is not whether a person experiences the future as mostly open. Rather, our discussion is whether humanity's future is unknown to God. Open theists have to prove that the future does not even exist in God's mind in the form of exhaustive information. Needless to say, this is a gigantic leap. Since we already have empirical evidence that God has predicted events in the distant future, open theists have their work cut out for them. Regardless of any conclusion we may draw, one thing is certain. God's relationship to the future cannot be ascertained by citing human experiences and limitations.

When Boyd stated that people's deliberations about the future must have real options in order to be genuine, he made an accurate description about *how* humans struggle with their decision-making

---

[95] Boyd, 144

process in the present time. The future is always uncertain for people. In reality, humans never experience the future. We always experience life as a persistent present tense. Thus, it is a fallacy to propose that freewill gives people the ability to alter their futures. The best that can be said on this issue is that people's present decisions influence tomorrow's course of events for them. That said, we also know that people do not know anything about the different external circumstances that will influence their decisions once they engage their environments. It's painfully obvious that if the future does not exist as a concrete reality for people, the best that can be said is that humans can take some actions in the present that could affect a future event. However, humanity's actions have nothing to say about God's knowledge of anything.

Boyd's second statement requires that, in order to have a genuine choice, we have to assume that "most of the future that surrounds the issue I am deliberating is predictable and not up to me to decide."[96] At the very minimun this statement is deceiving. Let us dissect it.

First, the future is never predictable for humans, unless they are talking about the predictability of the sun's rising. In this case, it is true that the future is predictable—the sun will rise tomorrow. But even this is deceiving because the person making the statement may not get to see the sun rise. In that case, the predictability of the sun's rising for that person will never become experientially true. Any guesswork we go through about tomorrow is always conditioned by the assumption that we will be alive tomorrow, which is a risky proposition at best.

Secondly, the phrase *"most of the future* that surrounds the issue I am deliberating" (emphasis added) is a bait-and-switch trick. The fact that people can deliberate *future issues*, as opposed to experiencing future events, has never been denied. However, since people cannot know future events, there cannot be an *actual future* surrounding an issue being deliberated in the present. That is, we can deliberate our future plans and their potential consequences, but we cannot discuss the actual future consequences surrounding an issue that does not yet exist for us.

---

[96] Boyd, 144.

I agree with the statement that people *need* to have a *genuinely open* future to be free. This is a necessary position to counter classical theology's view that God has already preordained every future human action. With the previous quote, Boyd brings us back to classical theology's deterministic motif. This is where open theists draw their line. However, while I agree with the statement in principle (the future is genuinely open to people because they have not made any decisions in the future because they don't live there), to suggest that this *need* also applies to God to a similar degree is patently false. After all, what does it mean for God to have a need for a "genuinely open" future? Is it possible for God to lose his *freedom* if he knows his own future? The suggestion that God is in a constant decision-making mode, weighing different alternatives in the present to shape the future, is not theologically defensible.

Additionally, it is not experientially true that people approach the future as partly settled and partly open. We *cannot experience* the future at all because we do not exist in the future. Our future is not only open; it is horrendously uncertain. People's futures can never be described as partly settled because their knowledge of the future can never be described as certain. The only time a person can speak of a certain future is if someone jumps from a plane without a parachute. He can speak of his future death while in midair. Thus, people's expectations about the future are always based on past knowledge or present experience—for example, the man is in midair without a parachute, and it is certain he will hit the ground very hard in a few seconds. Falling is the man's present reality. Hitting the ground is his future. The jumper can be certain of *that* future. We can predict the jumper's future based on experiential knowledge regarding the law of gravity. As the reader can notice, even this type of prediction is made based on present knowledge.

People's plans for the future settle nothing in the future for them. We are not even sure about our next breaths, much less any future behavior by people in an environment they do not control. It is also false to say that people experience the future as partly settled. The reality is that we can never experience the future at all. This line of reasoning does not even address the issue as it relates to God. Boyd gets lost in his own argument about our human limitations, then he extrapolates those limitations onto God, and he ends up with a fatal contradiction for his theological system.

Hasker sets forth a philosophical defense for open theology's view of the future. His argument uses the example of a man addicted to cheese omelets. He developed the argument as follows.

1) It is now true that Clarence will have a cheese omelet for breakfast tomorrow (premise). This is only true because the philosopher says it is true and not because there is any empirical evidence that this could in fact be true about Clarence's future.

2) It is impossible that God would at any time believe what is false or fails to believe anything that is true. (Premise: Divine Omniscience)

3) God has always believed that Clarence will have a cheese omelet tomorrow. (From 1, 2)

4) If God has always believed a certain thing, it is not in anyone's power to bring it about that God has not always believed that thing. (Premise: the un-alterability of the past)

5) Therefore, it is not in Clarence's power to bring it about that God has not always believed that he should have a cheese omelet for breakfast. (From 3, 4)

6) It is not possible to be true both that God has always believed that Clarence would have a cheese omelet for breakfast, and that he does not in fact have one. (From 2)

7) Therefore, it is not in Clarence's power to refrain from having a cheese omelet for breakfast tomorrow. (From 5, 6) So Clarence's eating the omelet tomorrow is not an act of free choice. (From the definition of freewill).[97]

Before we discuss the premises, one critical observation is in order. Hasker's initial premise is predicated upon Clarence's being alive

---

[97] Hasker, *The Openness of God*, 148.

tomorrow. Since neither Clarence nor Hasker knows as a matter of fact that Clarence will be alive tomorrow, Hasker's initial premise, "Clarence now knows that he will have a cheese omelet tomorrow," is false. The only thing that Clarence knows is that, since he normally has cheese omelets in the morning, if he is alive tomorrow, it is very likely that he will have a cheese omelet tomorrow. However, this probability says nothing about Clarence's actual knowledge about tomorrow. As such, the premise on which the entire argument is based is sketchy, making the rest of the argument unsustainable. However, for the sake of our discussion, let's play along.

First, God's knowledge of the future cannot be described as a belief (premises 2, 3, 4, 5, 6). Human beliefs have the tendency to be subjective. They usually depend on the information we have accumulated that supports the belief. Belief systems can be altered when new information is added. Before the year 1508 most people believed all the planets, including the sun, orbited around the earth. But all of that changed when Copernicus established a heliocentric solar system and determined that all the planets revolved around the sun.[98] God's knowledge cannot be described in these terms and at the same time sustain that whatever God knows is absolute. God either knows that Clarence will eat a cheese omelet, or he doesn't know. God's knowledge cannot be properly described as a belief. Beliefs are progressive and can change every time new information is added.

Second, what is true for Clarence today is not determinative of what will be true for him tomorrow. There is no direct cause and effect of anything Clarence does today that could predetermine what he will eat tomorrow. Clarence's house can burn to the ground, a tornado can destroy the house, or Clarence can develop a stomach virus and become unable to eat anything. There are so many variables that premise #1 is a logical possibility at best. We have already discussed that knowing possibilities is not real knowledge. Therefore, to describe God's knowledge of Clarence's habits as a "belief" that Clarence will eat a cheese omelet is ridiculous. If Clarence dies in the middle of the night, God's belief in Clarence's choice for breakfast is a moot point. If I say,

---

[98] Biography. Nicolaus Copernicus, (1473-1553). https://www.biography.com/people/nicolaus-copernicus-9256984

"I believe that if Clarence is alive tomorrow, he will eat a cheese omelet for breakfast," this is the flimsiest of all claims of knowledge.

Third, since Clarence's actual decision to eat the omelet will be made when tomorrow becomes his present, he does not have to fear God's knowledge of his decision because God already knows about Clarence's addiction to cheese omelets. If he made the decision to eat an omelet the night before, he can still change his mind in the morning. However, if Clarence makes his decision to eat a cheese omelet in the morning and God knew about his decision the previous day, Clarence is still free to make his choice regardless of God's knowledge. The one thing that cannot happen is for Clarence to make the decision to eat grits with cheese and for God to be surprised by this decision. Or, said another way, if God had revealed through a prophet that Clarence would eat a cheese omelet in the morning and Clarence ended up eating grits, God would be declared a liar. I do not think open theists want to continue down this road, especially when we consider Jowers's statement that God cannot guarantee his prophecies will come through.

Fourth, the premise that the inalterability of the past applies to the future as it relates to people is also false. Our knowledge of the past is based on verifiable, concrete events that have been experienced and recorded. While we cannot return to the past in a concrete form, (there is no such thing as time travel), we have physical evidence of past events. The nature of the future is, at best, conceptual without any historical reference. Humans cannot describe the future in language that implies certainty because they have no experiential or evidentiary documentation of it. For instance, I have never heard of an archaeologist digging for future evidence of an uncreated event.

The future does not have a historical point of reference for humanity, and this makes Hasker's reasoning a non-sequitur. The assumption that the nature of the future is identical to the past (premise 4, the inalterability of the past) is epistemologically false. And thus, his conclusion is irreparably incongruent with human experience and God's omniscience. Clarence's freedom is not altered by God's conceptual information regarding any or all of his choices. Clarence's actions tomorrow will be consistent with what he will choose when his future becomes his present. Therefore, his choice to eat an omelet will be freely made regardless of what God knows. However, Clarence's choice will also be consistent with God's knowledge.

Similarly, if I know about Clarence's predisposition to eat cheese omelets, my knowledge of his preferences is not a hindrance to his freedom to choose to eat cheese omelets. My knowledge is not determinative or causative for Clarence, and neither is God's. However, if Hasker could supply evidence of one instance in which God *believed* something to be true about a future event that turned out to be false, then his argument would be better grounded.

When the chips are down, open theists bring out their trump card—the claim that classical theology relies too much on pagan philosophy to support its principles. This accusation is not without merit, but that fact only confirms the deterministic flaw in classical theology, but it does not affirm open theism. I have heard many possible explanations that prove that Christmas is a pagan holiday, and—God forbid—we know that some pagans celebrated something on a day that we celebrate Jesus's birth. This is a suspect line of reasoning. The year has 365 days, and Jesus was born on one of those days. The chances that some pagan, somewhere, celebrated some pagan ritual on the same day of Jesus's birth are pretty good. Does that mean that we should never celebrate Jesus's birthday? This is ridiculous!

Boyd stated, "The main explanation for why so many assume that the future must be totally one way or the other ... is because of the vast influence of Plato in Western culture."[99] There are at least two possible refutations to Boyd's accusation. First, just because Plato, a pagan philosopher, had a vast influence on Western culture is not an argument against the legitimacy of the theological and philosophical foundation for God's omniscience. It is very possible that Plato had a legitimate argument to evaluate reality. But even if he didn't, the Bible still affirms God's capacity to "make the future known."

Second, Plato's influence is not determinative in matters of biblical interpretation, and it does not necessarily corrupt the process, even if it is true that Calvinism has been vastly influenced by Mani's

---

[99] Boyd, 144.

Gnosticism through St. Augustine's influence.[100] The Gnostic influence on St. Augustine did not focus on God's eternal attributes. H. Von Oort, Honorary Professor, Department of Church History, University of Pretoria, stated: "We even venture to say that, without a thorough knowledge of the 'Religion of Light' [Gnostic Manichaeism], Augustine's theology is hardly conceivable."[101] Von Oort's implication is that the Manichaean form of Gnosticism played a central role in Augustine's introduction of Gnosticism into Christian theology, especially as it relates to the doctrines of sin, freewill, and theological determinism. That Mani's Gnosticism influenced Augustine is not in doubt, but this influence does not invalidate all of Augustine's philosophy.

Boyd is correct in suggesting that classical theologians have too much dependency on pagan religion or philosophy, especially as it refers to soteriology. This is especially true in light of the openness theologians' dependence on philosophy to support their most significant premises. It appears that the classical view's understanding of God's omniscience is Plato's fault. But I believe it is not accurate to suggest that biblical scholars are incapable of reaching theological conclusions independently of Greek philosophy or pagan religions. If this were true, then how have open theists escaped Greek influence, or are they so pure that their superior intellect protects them? Plato's philosophical influence in classical theology, even if true, is not an argument against foreknowledge or in favor of the open view, especially since the concept of foreknowledge is clearly stated in the Bible (Acts 2:23; 1 Pet. 1:2).

Boyd said, "the classical view of God was decisively influenced by pagan philosophy."[102] Robert Nash answers this accusation by pointing out,

> What really troubles me about this allegation, that orthodox theology has been strongly influenced by Greek thought, is that in this particular case it is open theism that manifests the influence of Greek thinking. The idea of a finite God; that is the territory of Plato and Aristotle. If you're looking at least at the

---

[100] H von Oort. Augustine and Manicheism: New Discoveries, New Perspectives, (2005), p. 709

[101] Ibid.

[102] Boyd, 24.

idea that a supreme being cannot know the future, that comes directly from Aristotle. So far as I know that particular idea was originated by Aristotle in his book on interpretation.[103]

Not only does Nash answer the accusation that open theists throw at classical theologians, he also points to two specific instances in which open theists are guilty of doing what they allege classical theologians have done. We have already seen examples of this influence in open theism above. Open theists have basically adopted Cicero's definition of *foreknowledge* and applied it to theology.

In order for the open view's theological principles to work, their readers must accept the partly settled future concept without considering its ramifications on God's attributes. The inevitable conclusion is that an open future resides outside of God's scope of knowledge. Imagine that. God knows future events, but he does not know all the variables that makes those events possible. In order for God to partly settle a nonexistent reality, we need to blindly accept that God must have partial knowledge of something that not even he can know. How can they escape this conundrum? I submit to you that they cannot.

Boyd states that the God of the open view can predetermine some human behaviors and outcomes,[104] thus *he must believe that the God of the open view has, at times, foreknown uncreated human events*. Otherwise his statement about a partly settled future makes no sense. The partly settled future option makes it acceptable for God to violate human freewill from time to time. If human freewill is an absolute standard that cannot be violated, then God, who established it, should have no desire or reason to violate it.

Let me conclude this section by describing several logical and hermeneutical errors I have found in the theological and philosophical presuppositions of open theism.

1. They err in suggesting a cause-and-effect relationship between divine information (knowledge) and human freewill (ability to make moral choices without external compulsion). Since information exists in a

---

[103] Michael Collander, Interview with Ronald Nash. *Reformed Theological Seminary*, (2005).
[104] Boyd, 31.

realm different from the physical world, God's knowledge of the physical world is causative only when he chooses to act upon said knowledge. (Example: when he answers prayers)

2. They err in holding that God's creative activity confined him to a temporal understanding of time. Only an a priori assumption that accepts McCabe's nescient proposition can make this premise possible.

3. They err when they do not appear to take into account how humanity's fallen nature and natural laws influence and condition people's decision-making process.

4. They err when they assume that God's knowledge necessarily has to be defined from a temporal, linear point of view.

5. They err when they base their theology in the philosophical presupposition of God's nescience doctrine. There are no biblical passages that support McCabe's nescience doctrine or Basinger's present-knowledge doctrine.

The book of Deuteronomy establishes the credentials for a true prophet. Moses wrote,

> If what a prophet proclaims in the name of the LORD does not take place or come true, that is a message the LORD has not spoken. That prophet has spoken presumptuously. Do not be afraid of him. (Deut. 18:22)

God has revealed events, circumstances, and world affairs in a distant future. He has staked his reputation on those events taking place as predicted. The previous passage is a necessary and unqualified condition to identify a true prophet. How much more does Moses's prerequisite have to be true for the true God? Based on the biblical, prophetic test, the God of open theism does not meet the criterion of a true prophet. As you remember, Pinnock and Jowers have claimed that many prophecies have not been fulfilled. Thus, their implication is that God failed in his predictions.

This is not a minor problem because biblical prophecy is the one element that clearly separates God from idols. It is important to remember that all prophecy must, by necessity, include future uncreated human events and choices. If people's futures are unknowable to God, then any prophecy that includes human activity is outside of God's purview. Prophecy becomes a guessing game in which God will be wrong more often than right because seven billion people acting independently of his omniscience will see to it. The Bible is the only holy book in the world that contains accurate, consistent, and persistent prophetic utterances. Prophecy is one of the qualities that makes the Christian God unique. If God does not have the power to reveal the future, he cannot be trusted to fulfill his promises.

The prophetic issue is very complicated, but one thing is certain: prophecy is simply not possible without foreknowledge. In addition to that, God has expressly stated that he holds the exclusive capacity to predict the future.

God Knows What He Has Purposed

Another innovative concept put forth by open theists states that God's foreknowledge is limited to whatever he has purposed about himself. Boyd said it thus: "God foreknows that certain things are going to take place because he knows his own purpose and intentions."[105] In other words, God's foreknowledge is limited to his personal plans. In this sense, God is not any wiser than any person on earth because every single person alive foreknows his or her own purposes and intentions. The difference, I would venture to guess, is that we cannot make our plans come through, but God can force his way onto human affairs, and he can do as he pleases, as long as it's congruent with his character.

Boyd's logic requires that God's foreknowledge not be any better than humanity's. Open theism needs to explain what God has purposed and revealed about himself that does not include a relationship with people. Asked differently, is there anything God has purposed that does not have humanity as the object of his revelation? Boyd does not even address this issue. This is the problem with his statement: since

---

[105] Boyd, 30.

God's revelation and activity on this earth has always been in relationship with people, there is nothing God can purpose for himself that excludes human involvement.

Boyd added, "God predestines and foreknows as settled whatever he sees fit to predestine and foreknow as settled."[106] The open view cannot logically propose that God foreknows and settles anything he wants while at the same time declaring that God cannot foreknow anything in the future that relates to people *because* it has told us in no uncertain terms that the human future does not exist. If God can predestine anything he chooses, then Boyd is overstating the obvious and defeating his own foundational premise that the future does not exist. If God can foreknow and settle whatever he wants, then it follows that he could choose to know and settle every single event in the future because he can choose to know anything he wants. However, if Boyd is arguing that God can partly settle people's futures without knowing what they will do, then he is defending an irreconcilable contradiction that cannot be brushed over.

The open view's objections to foreknowledge are nonsensical for two reasons. First, as stated in the previous paragraph, they advance the proposition that God can indeed foreknow and settle anything he wants. If this is true, then the classical view of foreknowledge is correct, and the open view is a smoke screen. Second, if in spite of the previous statement, open view theologians argue that God can settle the future without knowing that future, then they must believe that God can act against his own nature. This is simply preposterous.

We need to point out that our present debate is not about God's ability to move rocks or replant trees. The present discussion's relevance is connected to the all-important dichotomy of divine sovereignty and human freedom. Therefore, to speak of God's ability to partly settle what he has purposed is a nonissue. God's ability to make and settle his own plans has never been opposed by anyone. The issue is the open view's claim that God can partly settle future human activity in light of its fundamental premise that future human activity does not exist and cannot be known even by God.

---

[106] Boyd, 53.

Additionally, no one has ever questioned God's ability to know his own thinking. The question is whether God's thinking includes foreknowledge of future human choices. Therefore, to speak of what God has purposed is a diversion. The claims that God does not have foreknowledge of human activity and that he has enough foreknowledge to partly settle selective future human events are incongruent. What is the basis that could reconcile these two contradictory statements? How does God decide which events he will predestine if he does not know any of them? If God is free to choose the events he will predestine, does not this imply that he has the power and knowledge to predestine *every* event? Does not this also imply that God selects a few events for predestination while leaving others untouched? But how can God choose to predestine some and not others *if He cannot know whether those events are contingent upon each other*?

Let me ask a few additional questions here. What could be considered partial knowledge for a perfect God? Does God know only some aspects of the events in the future he has partly settled, or is he just settling some events without actually knowing them? How does God partly know these events if the future actions of free agents do not exist for him to know?[107] Does God have full knowledge of the event he has chosen to partly settle, or does he just have partial knowledge of the event itself? Or is God able to foreknow events he has purposed and caused to happen that are divorced and independent of human involvement?

God's partial knowledge of a future event must have a negative impact on his ability to accurately predict the event itself because the event has other contingencies and correlated events that influence it. If we say that God knows 40 percent of the possibility that an airplane will land at Atlanta airport before noon, this knowledge is insufficient for God to predict the event's outcome. Even if God had 90 percent knowledge of all of the possibilities for a particular event, he could not make an accurate prediction. There is still a 10 percent chance that he might be wrong, and this is too much of a gamble for a perfect God. There are too many variables for God to partly settle any particular event.

---

[107] Boyd, 17.

One of the most fundamental premises of the open view requires that all divine knowledge be contingent upon events created by people, and since human events do not exist to be known, then God cannot partly settle any future event that has human involvement—turning biblical prophecy on its head. If all biblical prophecy is directly connected to human activity on earth in relationship to God's divine will, and if God cannot know future human events, then by definition, prophecy is outside God's purview. The open view cannot escape this conclusion; thus, it must reject one of God's most significant attributes as spelled out in Isaiah 48:14 ("Who among them has declared these things?"). God is worthy of worship because he is different from idols, and he alone can make the future known.

How can God settle his own future actions in relationship to people if his actions are connected to uncreated and unknowable human events? Or does God only know his side of events with no connection to the external world of human acts? The God of the open view cannot purpose actions that he cannot know. The logical gymnastics required to explain the partly settled/partly open future concepts in relationship to what God has purposed are unnerving.

God Knows All Possibilities

Boyd uses the example of a cosmic chess player to describe God's ability to know all possibilities. I am an amateur chess player myself, and when I play, I always try to guess five or six plays that my opponent might be considering as a response to my plays. Obviously, I do not know all the possibilities. However, even my ability to know the possibilities of a few plays does not mean that I can be certain of what the other player will do. God's knowledge of all possibilities in the cosmic chess game would make sense if there were another player. But such a player does not exist.

Freewill is not God's opponent because he created freewill to function within his creative activity. To claim that God can know a million moves that span a few days is one thing. Even I can know a limited number of moves. But to say that God's ability to guess trillions upon trillions of possibilities that may or may not occur is actual knowledge is ridiculous. The greater the number of possibilities is, the smaller is the chance to accurately guess an outcome. We properly call this gambling. Gamblers buy a lottery ticket on the possibility that their numbers will come up. They know one possibility. Sometimes their numbers do come up. But no serious, thinking person can take this chaotic and unlikely guess and call it knowledge. Let me expand on this.

If one person flips a coin, there are two possibilities, heads or tail. In this case God has a fifty-fifty chance to correctly predict which side of the coin will land facing up. Similarly, the odds of a person correctly guessing the flip of a coin are fifty-fifty. The odds of guessing 100 coins flips is always fifty-fifty for anyone flip. However, the odds of that same person guessing correctly 100 consecutive flips of a coin are one with thirty zeroes following it (10^{30} power). If we expand that to say that seven billion people are making seven billion decisions per second, the odds that the God of the possible can make the right guess about anything are greater than a number that has not yet been invented.

The fact that God knows all those trillions and trillions of possibilities says nothing about God's knowledge. God will not be surprised by any decisions that people make, but this is a far cry from saying he knew anything about the decisions themselves. Since the God of open theism cannot know future events because they have not been created, we have to conclude that the God of open theism does not know anything about the future or even the present. What if the opposing player makes a dumb mistake and decides to add a different move before the anticipated move? It throws the whole scheme into chaos. If truly knowing the very next move is extremely unpredictable, how will the God of open theism connect moves that would take place a hundred years from now by people who have not yet been born? In other words, the God of open theism cannot risk making any prophecies about a person's future because nothing in a person's future can be known with any degree of certainty, even if God knows all the possibilities.

The God of Foreknowledge Is Less Wise

Boyd also suggests that the God of foreknowledge is *less wise* than the God of the open view.[108] What is the evidence that supports this

---

[108] Boyd, 128.

assertion? He expands on the chess game analogy. He stated, "One [player] beats a computerized chessboard because he knows how it was programmed and thus knows every move it *will* make. The other beats a person by anticipating every possible move he *might* make. Which one is a more praise-worthy champion?"[109] It is difficult to put into words the inadequacy of this analogy.

Let me get this straight. God, who created the chessboard (or the universe) and knows how the game is played, is not playing a smart game because he knows how the "computerized chessboard" he created will make every move. But if God had created the universe without knowing how the game he had just created would be played, then he would be wiser. He has to be kidding! Boyd is actually suggesting that God has to win his own game by using his ingenuity to beat himself without knowing how his computerized chessboard will make its moves. So, God's victory would be more praiseworthy if he had created the game in such a way that not even he would know how the game would unfold. What kind of logic is this? Who exactly would be praising God's ingenuity? Or why would God need ingenuity to win at his own game? This is bizarre.

Let us consider two options to this cosmic chess game. First, according to Boyd, the God of foreknowledge should not have created the universe in a way that he has an unfair advantage. Question: Against whom is this unfair advantage? Boyd suggests that since God is the player who created the chessboard and knows all its moves, he is not as praiseworthy as the player (the god of open theism?) who outguesses his allegorical chessboard opponent (human freewill?). I don't know what this allegory is trying to prove. One thing is clear. Boyd cannot shake off his Calvinistic past and continues to create new ways to defeat the ghost of determinism.

Second, Boyd could be suggesting that the God of open theism (the wiser description of God) is outguessing himself in the cosmic chess game. I really hope that Boyd is not saying that God has to outguess himself. That would be really sad. He stated that the player who beats a competitor is clearly smarter.[110] I guess we must assume

---

[109] Boyd, 128
[110] Ibid, 128

that human freewill is God's opponent in the cosmic chess game. Therefore, based on Boyd's logic, God created human freewill, so he could play a cat-and-mouse game to prove that he is smart enough to win a game without knowing its outcome. A quote from the psalmist is appropriate here: "What is man that you are mindful of him, and the son of man that you care for him?" (Ps. 8:4). The psalmist's question implies that, in comparison to God, humanity is nothing, and yet the Lord has remembered them. Are people God's opponents on the cosmic chess game? I don't think so.

Apparently, Boyd is advancing the novel idea that God can only be smarter than *the other player,* whoever he might be, if he did not create the universe—the so-called computerized chessboard—with a built-in advantage to himself. How should God have created the chessboard? Since there is only one Creator of the universe, it is more reasonable to assume that he knows everything there is to know about the universe than to believe that the God of open theism has to somehow outguess some fictional cosmic character (freewill) to accomplish his will. Please! Are they serious? How is it possible that the God who designed and created the entire computerized galactic chess game be less wise than the God of open theism playing a game that he is utterly unprepared to win?

Biblical Prophecy

Let us examine the issue of biblical prophecy more closely. As we discussed earlier, the book of Deuteronomy established the credentials for a true prophet, by saying that if a prophet proclaims something that doesn't prove true, that was not a message from the Lord.

Boyd stated, "While the Bible portrays the crucifixion as a predestined event, it never suggests that the individuals who participated in this event were predestined to do so or foreknown as doing so."[111] Let me make a few comments regarding this quote.

First, the Bible does not *portray* the crucifixion as a predestined event. It *clearly states* that it was a predestined event (Eph. 1:35; Heb.

---

[111] Boyd, 45.

9:26; 1 Pet. 1:20). Each one of these passages makes reference to God's plan in Jesus since before the foundation of the world. Second, since the crucifixion was a predestined event, God must have known the exact year, day, and hour in which it was going to take place. And in order to know the year, he must also have known the political, social, and religious conditions that would make the crucifixion a fixed event in his mind. Since Jesus was the divine sacrificial lamb, the crucifixion had to take place on Passover. This is very specific knowledge. Additionally, God predestined the crucifixion before this method of execution was invented. As the prophecies were given, no one could have guessed the context that would produce crucifixions as an execution method for criminals. In order to make such a prediction, God must have foreknown that at some point in history this execution method would be used as a form of punishment. Also, he must have known the political, cultural, and religious conditions that would bring about Jesus's crucifixion.

Additionally, he must have been able to foresee every sequence in the chain of events that led to Jesus's crucifixion because a crucifixion cannot take place in a historical vacuum. This sequence of events must have included the knowledge that every person in Jesus's lineage would survive to ensure Jesus's birth from Mary.

Third, Boyd suggested that God was absolutely certain that Jesus would be crucified but that God did not know anything about the surrounding events, or the people associated with the crucifixion. It is simply not possible for God to be certain about Jesus's crucifixion, a human event, without knowing the people involved or the circumstances that led to the event itself. If the crucifixion is a human event, and it is, then the event cannot be understood independently of the circumstances that made it possible. But it is worse than that. Since the crucifixion is a human event, the God of open theism could not have predicted that it would happen because the event did not exist to be known until it became a historical reality. Even if we concede that God would send Jesus to the world at a particular time, Jesus was not going to crucify himself. Other people had to do that, and God had to have known those people's willingness to carry out the crucifixion. Otherwise, God could have sent Jesus to earth to later find out that people were not ready to crucify him.

Finally, Boyd stated, "It was not certain from eternity that Pilate, Herod, or Caiaphas would play the roles they played in the crucifixion."[112] Apparently, Boyd wants a "by name" prophetic roster of every person involved in the crucifixion. The fact that those names are not included in the prophecy does not mean that God did not know them. The names were withheld precisely to guarantee their freewill. As a matter of fact, we have at least two instances in which God predicted the names of people who would be born. Consider this prediction.

> By the word of the LORD a man of God came from Judah to Bethel, as Jeroboam was standing by the altar to make an offering. He cried out against the altar by the word of the LORD: "O altar, altar! This is what the LORD says: 'A son named ***Josiah*** will be born to the house of David. On you he will sacrifice the priests of the high places who now make offerings here, and human bones will be burned on you.'" That same day the man of God gave a sign: "This is the sign the LORD has declared: The altar will be split apart and the ashes on it will be poured out." (1 Kgs. 13:1–3)

The second passage is found in Isaiah's prophecy that took place about seven hundred years before Christ. His prophecy was remarkable in that it predicted the birth and the reign of a Gentile king whom God would use as an instrument to rebuild the city of Jerusalem. The reader needs to keep in mind that Isaiah's prophecy was given before Jerusalem had been destroyed.

> Who says of Cyrus, "He is my shepherd and will accomplish all that I please; he will say of Jerusalem, "Let it be rebuilt," and of the temple, "Let its foundations be laid." (Is. 44:28)

These two prophecies provide definite evidence that God knew the specific names of at least two people who would be born in the future. Not only that, but God gave specific information about these individuals' mission. If God could name Josiah and Cyrus, why could he not name Pilate and Judas? He could have, but he chose not to. And the rest, as they say, is history. For Boyd to claim that "it was not certain from eternity" that God knew these players' names and roles is

---

[112] Boyd, 45.

presumptuous at best. If God could know Josiah and Cyrus, what could prevent him from knowing Judas, Pilate, and Caiaphas?

Boyd also made reference to these two passages.[113] He stated, "The decree obviously set parameters around the freedom of the parents in naming these individuals."[114] The reader needs to remember that Boyd is the man who told us that God cannot know uncreated events. He does not explain how the God of the open view can set parameters for the parents of two individuals that would become kings hundreds of years in the future. The God of the open view cannot predetermine the birth of two future kings to be born at the precise time they needed to be born to accomplish specific purposes, without knowing *all* the events that led to their births. These two individuals were born to two distinct societies and cultures under very different circumstances.

The issue is not limited to God's selection of the names of people in the far-off future. That is difficult enough. The God of open theism does not have a mechanism to know who Cyrus's parents would be, much less that Cyrus himself would become a Persian general who would rise to defeat the Babylonian army and become king. The Babylonian Empire did not even exist yet. Boyd has the tendency to dismiss evidence in a cavalier fashion without considering all the possible implications of his statements. The naming of Josiah and Cyrus is a more complicated matter than Boyd would have us believe, especially when we consider how complicated it is to predict the restoration of Israel by a world power different from the power that conquered them in the first place and before the initial conquest had taken place! Israel was not even close to captivity when the prophecy was given. How could the God of open theism pick a name out of a hat for someone who would be born more than one hundred fifty years later to be king of a pagan nation? Sorry, but I do not buy the "God predestined this event out of thin air" rationale. The God of the open view, as defined by Boyd, cannot do this.

No one knows what God knows from eternity past, except God himself. Consider Peter's words related to Jesus's crucifixion from eternity: "Knowing that you were ransomed from the futile ways

---

[113] Boyd, 34.
[114] Ibid.

inherited from your forefathers, not with perishable things such as silver or gold, but with the precious blood of Christ, like that of a lamb without blemish or spot. *He was foreknown before the foundation of the world* but was made manifest in the last times for the sake of you" (1 Pet. 1:18–20, emphasis added). Open theists may not know what God was thinking before the foundation of the world, but Peter tells us that God foreknew the cross in eternity past.

However, if Boyd has specific information, "from eternity," that God does not have, he should present his evidence. Otherwise, his statement is just another wild speculation that cannot be taken seriously. That said, to suggest that God predestined the crucifixion in a historical vacuum is not theological or logically sound. If God predestined Jesus's crucifixion from eternity, it follows that he must have also known the time, the place, the players, and the circumstances that would bring this event to fruition.

God knew that Jesus's side would be pierced (Is. 53:5). A man who did not know about the prophecy did the piercing. This event happened while Jesus was defenseless, hanging on the cross. Jesus could not have orchestrated this event. The piercing of Jesus's side was a purely human event that the God of the open view could not have known seven hundred years earlier. This also means that God predicted this human event related to Jesus that did not include any action on Jesus's part. It appears that God knew more than seven hundred years before the crucifixion that one of the soldiers would pierce Jesus's side. We should also note that Isaiah described the event in the past tense— "he was pierced." By the time Isaiah uttered the prophecy, as far as God was concerned, the piercing of Jesus's side was as good as done.

Types of Prophecies

There are two basic types of biblical prophecies, the conditional and the unconditional. The conditional prophecy is always contingent upon some human response to God's revelation. The operative word for conditional prophecies is *if.* This type of prophecy always adds a prerequisite before the promises or curses are fulfilled. In other words, before the promised blessing can be received, the recipient must do something. However, the fact that a conditional prophecy is given does not mean that God does not know what the people will, in fact, choose. One example of a conditional prophecy is when God told the people,

> "Now *if you obey me fully and keep my covenant,* then out of all nations you will be my treasured possession. Although the whole earth is mine, you will be for me a kingdom of priests and a holy nation." These are the words you are to speak to the Israelites. (Ex. 19:5–6)

In spite of the conditional nature of this statement, 1,400 years before Christ was born, God still predicted that the Messiah would come out of the people of Israel because God's covenant with Abraham superseded Israel's obedience through the law (Gen. 15:1–21). In other words, God would make Israel his treasured possession if they obeyed, but the fact that he promised Jesus's birth from Israel's ancestry fully assured that Israel would be the recipient of the promise made in his covenant with Abraham.

The unconditional prophecy, however, does not have any prerequisites for its fulfillment. In this type of prophecy, God reveals the future, and there is nothing people can do to change its fulfillment. The *if* is not attached to it. The following is an example of an unconditional prophecy.

> I, Daniel, was troubled in spirit, and the visions that passed through my mind disturbed me. I approached one of those standing there and asked him the true meaning of all this. So he told me and gave me the interpretation of these things: "The four great beasts are four kingdoms that will rise from the earth. But the saints of the Most High will receive the kingdom and will possess it forever—yes, for ever and ever." (Dan. 7:15–18)

Open theism suggests that God knows the general elements of future events but not the details.[115] How could the God of open theism know that four political and military kingdoms (not five, seven, or three) would rise if he did not know how humans would establish them? This prophecy is so precise that it has baffled unbelievers for centuries. The passage does not say that if all the stars line up in the right order, four kingdoms have the possibility of rising from the earth. The prophecy

---

[115] Boyd, 40.

could not have been more specific— "Four kingdoms *will* rise from the earth." Knowing all the possibilities would not have been sufficient to make this prophecy.

The Open View's Prophetic Dilemma

Prophecy, by its very definition, is the ability to accurately predict future events. The Bible is full of examples in which God's predictions of future human activity are validated and verified. If prophecy is to be properly understood, God must have, at the very least, a cognitive awareness of future human events. The narrative found in Scripture is a description of humanity's response to God's revelation, in both its historical and its prophetic contexts. Biblical prophecy is the written affirmation that God has foreknowledge regarding human future activity.

The more precise the prediction is, *the clearer* is the picture God wants to communicate. Often, we need a hindsight view of historical events to grasp God's revelation. Since prophecy is related to God's knowledge of the future, a higher degree of specificity regarding the event predicted results in a clearer picture for us. Of course, *prophetic clarity* is a relative term that we use in our attempt to understand God's revelations. However, *prophetic clarity* cannot be a relative term to God as it relates to his foreknowledge. God's revelation of people's futures cannot be a muddled picture of possibilities to him. Since God is perfect, whatever he foreknows must also be perfect.

For example, as we have already seen, Daniel's vision of the four kingdoms was a very precise prophecy. God did not reveal the geopolitical details that would have been necessary to produce each kingdom, and it is also very probable that Daniel did not have a clue as to how much God knew about the details that would result in the prophecy's fulfillment. Daniel did not have enough information to understand a world that resided beyond his personal circumstances, and God did not fill in the blanks for him. The details belong to God. Daniel's prophecy was as detailed as Daniel could have understood it, but people are not able to foresee all the variables involved in their fulfillment.

If God does not know the future, his prediction of the emergence of entire empires—with all the political, sociological, and historical consequences—had to be one of the most astounding gambles ever undertaken. Even though Daniel could not grasp the extent of his own prophecy, he trusted that God was not misleading him.

The explanation, "that God has settled whatever he has chosen to settle,"[116] is insufficient to explain God's foreknowledge for the reasons given above. Open theists cannot have it both ways. To argue that God could predict the establishment of future kingdoms, with all the complexity that entails, in the precise order of their appearance without knowing how they would come to pass is foolish. The God of open theism cannot predict events that include human variances and uncertainties, regardless of what open theists say about the partly settled future concept. We will now consider Boyd's specific example of Jesus's prediction of Peter's denial.

Peter's Denial

Boyd proposes that Jesus predicted Peter's denials without knowing any of the details that made them possible.[117] According to Boyd, Jesus's prediction was solely based on his knowledge of a flaw in Peter's character. Let us read Boyd's description of the event.

> Contrary to the assumption of many, we do not need to believe that the future is exhaustively settled to explain this prediction. We only need to believe that God the Father knew and revealed to Jesus one very predictable aspect of Peter's character.[118]

I believe Boyd moved too quickly from Jesus's prediction of Peter's denial to Peter's restoration (Jn. 21:15–19) because he did not have any significant information to share about the denials themselves. This was a significant hermeneutical mistake. There is nothing in Jesus's prediction that could have led anyone to believe that Peter's restoration was forthcoming. This is especially true in light of open theism's premise that God cannot know the future because it does not exist to be

---

116 Boyd, 52.
117 Ibid, 35.
118 Ibid, 35.

known. Boyd's own theology does not allow for God to cause Peter's denials with a future intent of restoration. The God of the open view cannot know any future human events, and both Peter's denials and his restoration were human events still in the future. In jumping to the conclusion of Peter's restoration, Boyd states, "Three times Peter had his true character squeezed out of him so that, after the resurrection, he might three times have Jesus's character squeezed into him."[119]

This is very cute, but Jesus could not have predicted Peter's denial in order to "squeeze" his character back into him later. This is nonsense. Boyd cannot assume that Jesus would anticipate Peter's restoration because he had no way of knowing Peter's reaction to the three denials. Actually, the two events can only be connected by the open view in hindsight. Peter's denials were predicted as a stand-alone event— "Before the rooster crows you will deny me three times" (Matt. 26:75).

Since the God of open theism could not have known Peter's ultimate reaction to the guilt the denials would cause him, his restoration could not have been the *reason* for the God of open theism to arrange the circumstances that produced his denials. The God of the open view could not have "orchestrated" the events surrounding the denials because this would have required the manipulation of people's freewill to achieve his purpose. Besides, the God of open theism could not have had Peter's restoration in mind because, as open theists have told us, prophecies often do not always come through. This is simply not possible within open view theology because future events are not there to be known.

However, if Peter's restoration *was* God's endgame, then God knew more about all the events surrounding the denials than Boyd is willing to concede. As a matter of application, Peter's denials made his restoration necessary, but to understand these two separate events as interconnected is not theologically sound. Classical view theologians have no problem seeing the events as connected because they have a deterministic worldview, as wrongheaded as that might be. However, the God of open theism has no such option.

---

[119] Boyd, 36.

If we accept Boyd's explanation, the God of open theism is able to predict a series of unconnected events (everything that happened that night from Jesus's arrest to the rooster's crowing), with thousands of variables, based on one man's character trait. The God of open theism has to be able to make this prediction even though the future of said man does not exist and cannot be known. This same God could not use his knowledge of Suzanne's husband's character to predict the betrayal (see Chapter Two). The apostle's cowardice, we are told, caused him to deny Jesus not only once, but three times.[120] If the God of open theism is able to make such a prediction in a contextual vacuum with Peter, he should have been able to give Suzanne similar warnings regarding her husband's inclination to unfaithfulness. Why wasn't the God of open theism able to reveal to Suzanne, based on his perfect knowledge of her husband's character, that the man she fell in love with was a scoundrel? Why does Boyd rush to such an easy explanation in Peter's case while ignoring the same possibility entirely in Suzanne's case?

One more thing needs to be made very clear. While the God of the open view may have desired to restore Peter at a later time, he could not have desired Peter's restoration until after the denials because he could not have known the effect the denials would have on Peter. Since open theists have told us that prophecies are not always fulfilled, the God of open theism could not have been certain that Peter would, in fact, deny Jesus three times. As far as Peter was concerned, the consequences of his denials could have been disastrous. Additionally, Boyd has stated that the God of the open view does not know uncreated events. Therefore, the God of the open view could not have made a connection between Peter's denials and his restoration. This is especially true because Boyd cannot simply explain away Peter's denials based on *a posteriori* reinterpretation of his restoration.

Let us consider another aspect of these events. The God of foreknowledge knew about Peter's restoration because he knew of Peter's love for Jesus and foreknew his sincere repentance. Jesus specifically told Peter, "Satan demanded to have you, that he might sift you like wheat, but I have prayed for you that your faith may not fail" (Lk. 22:31—32a ESV). Not only did Jesus know that Peter would deny

---

[120] Boyd, 36.

him, he also knew that the devil himself had asked God for permission to sift Peter. But Jesus had prayed for Peter, possibly so that he would not end up like Judas. The God of the open view could have planned Peter's restoration, but since he only knows the possibilities, there was no way for the God of openness to know that Peter would repent. Judas's guilt led him to suicide. Peter's guilt led him to repentance. How could the God of the open view plan Peter's restoration in light of what we know about Judas's reaction? What if Peter had responded like Judas? God knew a great deal more about these events than Boyd wants us to believe.

Boyd also stated,

> Anyone *who knew* Peter's character perfectly could have predicted that under *certain highly pressured* circumstances (that God could easily orchestrate), he would act just the way he did. [Emphasis added][121]

Let us dissect this quote. Boyd takes Jesus's prediction of the denial from the realm of the miraculous and places it in the realm of the routine. We cannot just dismiss his assertion as a minor presumption on Boyd's part. Boyd does not go into detail about what "the highly pressured circumstances" could be, but since the events included future uncreated human events, we have to speculate that Boyd must be referring to people's freewill. Is Boyd suggesting that God violated people freewill to ensure that Peter's denials occurred?

However, if the God of openness could not be absolutely sure that Peter would be present around the campfire that evening, there could not have been enough orchestrating to guarantee the prophecy's fulfillment. We need to understand that the God of the open view cannot "orchestrate" future human events without manipulating present human behavior. Therefore, Boyd must be advancing the novel idea that the God of open theism has to manipulate people's freewill to achieve his ends, effectively negating people's freewill.

What were the so-called highly pressured circumstances? Is Boyd suggesting that God coerced Peter and the three questioners to attend the campfire? Is he suggesting that God coerced three curious

---

[121] Boyd, 35.

people to pick Peter out of the crowd in order to question him based on God's planting the question in their heads? If Boyd is suggesting that God controlled their behavior, then all his speechifying about freewill is nothing more than meaningless rhetoric. Let us remember that while it is true that God could have planned these circumstances—after all, he has all the power in the universe—what does that say about the God of the open view's lack of respect for human freewill?

It is very disconcerting to read that the God of open theism was "orchestrating circumstances" to pressure Peter into three denials. The only circumstances that God could have orchestrated were the manipulation of other people's freewill. If this is what Boyd has in mind, then he is contradicting one of the most fundamental premises in open theism—that God does not violate libertarian freewill. Since the God of the open view does not know the "future actions of future free agents," it is not reasonable to expect that he could orchestrate circumstances that would lead to events that did not exist at the moment that Jesus made his prediction.

In order for the God of open theism to accomplish his goal to cause Peter's denials, he would have had to manipulate the present circumstances and the freewill of the following people: (1) the guards so that they would not strike back at Peter and kill him after Peter had attacked one of them, (2) the three questioners so that they would attend the trial and choose to ask a similar question of a stranger in the middle of the night, (3) Peter to make him attend the trial even though the other disciples had fled, (4) the one disciple who accompanied Peter, who by an incredible coincidence was friends with the high priest, and (5) the girl who allowed Peter to enter the courtyard.

I do not believe the three questioners, the girl at the door, the unidentified person in John 18:25, and the relative of the guard whose ear Peter had cut off, were involved in a conspiracy, orchestrated by Jesus, against Peter. I also do not believe that the actions by all those players can be explained through Peter's character flaw. Their interaction with Peter was not knowable to the God of open theism until the events were created at the precise moment of their encounter with Peter. And yet each person conveniently followed the script that Jesus laid out and acted within the parameters of the prediction. Were their characters predisposed to ask questions to a stranger in the middle of the night regarding his relationship to a man who had been brought to trial—all based on Peter's character flaw?

It is curious that Boyd, who has dedicated a book to protecting human freewill, could so easily concede that the God of the open view would "orchestrate the circumstances" to facilitate Peter's denial. Boyd cannot bring himself to say that God manipulated people's freewill, but those are the only circumstances that matter here. He certainly cannot be talking about the manipulation of the weather. There is only one explanation for Jesus's prediction of the three denials. God had "exhaustively settled" information about the event, and he must have known how the evening's events would unfold. God was so sure of Peter's upcoming denials that Jesus made an absolute prediction about them, not a conditional one. If Boyd wants us to take his theory seriously, he needs to come up with an exposition that includes specific details to explain how Peter's character flaw was sufficient to determine the outcome of more than six hours of interactions between countless free moral agents totally unrelated to one another. He also needs to explain how Peter's character flaw influenced the timing of the rooster's crowing. Peter's denials were not one event, but a chain of events with multiple players and thousands of possibilities that concluded with the rooster's crowing.

Boyd hastily decides that everything that happened that night, including the rooster crowing at the precise moment of Peter's last denial, can be explained away as a flaw in Peter's character. While this may be a convenient explanation for the open view, I think it is purely wishful thinking. If any of the above-mentioned events would have failed to occur, Jesus would have been declared a false prophet just before his death. And open theists do not think this is significant!

The Character Flaw Argument

Self-preservation is a paramount human need, even if it is achieved through a cowardly act. Probably ninety-nine percent of the people on this earth would choose to run when facing a life-threatening danger. The disciples felt that their lives were in danger and they fled, even though they would have preferred to stay. Peter stayed close enough to Jesus that he was identified as one of Jesus's followers, even though his heart was filled with fear. Peter's fear was not enough to send him running away from Jesus.

We have to remember that Jesus not only predicted that Peter *could* deny him. He predicted that, in fact, he *would* deny him. Jesus's challenge must have been a powerful motivator for Peter to follow Jesus, without realizing that the pressure would eventually overtake his desire to stay with his Savior. God must have known Peter well enough to know that he would follow Jesus in spite of his fears, and he revealed to Jesus the final result of Peter's inner struggle. It is possible that Jesus did not know all the details, but it is impossible for the Father not to have known them. Let's look at a few items God must have known about that night.

- God must have known—and revealed to Jesus—that the arrest and an illegal trial would take place that night, thus the prophecy: "Before the rooster crows, you will deny me three times."

- God must have known that three different people would question Peter's association with Jesus and that those questions would lead to Peter's denials during a specific time frame

- A disciple who knew the high priest would make it possible for Peter to enter the high priest's courtyard

- A relative of the man whose ear Peter had cut off would identify Peter around the campfire

- Peter would not run away after the first or second denials

The reader needs to understand that any prophecy without a historical context is meaningless. Open theists cannot simply ignore the thousands, or even millions, of variables and possibilities that were interconnected with this event that could have changed the outcome.

Peter's character flaw is, at best, only one of the variables that Jesus had to account for in his prediction. Even a well-educated guess by Jesus could not guarantee that three people, unrelated to one another, with their own set of character flaws would interact with Peter and provoke him into denying Jesus. Peter's character flaw does not account for the fact that the other disciple knew the high priest and that, upon his request, the high priest would agree to let Peter in the courtyard. The God of open theism could not have connected all the events leading to the denials solely based on Peter's character.

Additionally, the God of openness could not have been certain that Jesus would be arrested that night. The open view's proponents' theological presuppositions exclude this possibility because uncreated events do not exist to be known, in their view. The arrest itself was an uncreated event until it actually happened, even though Jesus acted as if he was sure that he was going to be arrested and tried that night. He arranged for the Last Supper days in advance and celebrated with the disciples the same night of the arrest. During the supper, Jesus encouraged Judas to finish the evil work he had begun (Jn. 13:27). Judas must have made the deal with the religious leaders before the Last Supper. Otherwise, Jesus could not have scheduled the supper. Even if Jesus knew these details, how could the God of openness predict that Peter would deny Jesus that very night? This is simply not possible with openness theology.

I grant that Judas might have received the thirty pieces of silver before the supper and that the mob had begun to gather. But the God of open theism could not have guaranteed the arrest for that night. The Sanhedrin could have reconsidered the order, especially since they might have been concerned with violence just before Passover. Open theism simply does not have the necessary theological principles to assure us that Jesus could have known that his own arrest would have taken place that night with enough time for Peter to deny him before the rooster crowed, much less that Peter would be present at the campfire.

Boyd does not tell us anything about Jesus's perfect knowledge regarding the character qualities of the three questioners or the other disciple who accompanied Peter or regarding how Peter's character flaw influenced the high priest to give the order for the arrest. What would have happened if the high priest had waited until after Passover? How can their character flaws assist us in understanding Peter's denial? Boyd says nothing about them, in spite of the fact that they are critical for Jesus's prediction. God could not have revealed to Jesus such a momentous prediction without considering the pertinent variables.

Peter, the Courageous

I find Boyd's characterization of Peter as a coward[122] to be inaccurate and not supported by the evidence. I agree that Peter experienced fear, but I do not agree that experiencing fear makes a person a coward. A coward would not have picked a fight with the well-trained Roman soldiers and temple guards. Peter actually attacked the servant of the high priest. Furthermore, a coward would not have followed Jesus to the courtyard and entered it, especially after he had attempted to kill the priest's servant. And a coward would not have stayed in the courtyard after he was identified as one of Jesus's followers.

Boyd erroneously identifies Peter's aggression against the soldiers who came to arrest Jesus as "superficial bravado."[123] According to the biblical record, Peter pulled his sword during the arrest and attacked the high priest's servant (Matt. 26:51; Jn. 18:10). It takes more than a fake act of aggression to pull a sword against a military company and physically attack those well-armed and trained guards who would not have hesitated to retaliate with deadly force. Imagine if one of them had killed Peter during the attack. Jesus would not have been much of a prophet. Peter was ready to die for Jesus. *What Peter was not ready to do was die without a fight.* Boyd interprets the passage as if the variables were unnecessary and irrelevant nuances to Jesus's prediction. Boyd makes a major mistake when he ignores the numerous circumstances that were not connected to Peter's character that nevertheless played a key role in the prophecy.

We know some of Peter's character qualities. Peter was impulsive in his actions, and many times he spoke too quickly. When Jesus approached the disciples walking on water, Peter did not allow his fear to stop him from walking toward Jesus on the water (Matt. 14:29–30). Was Peter impulsive? Yes. Was his faith shaken when he realized that he was walking on water? Absolutely. Does that make him a coward? Not in a million years. Could he have acted cowardly at some point of his life? Possibly. Was cowardice a defining character trait for Peter? Absolutely not.

---

122 Boyd, 36.
123 Ibid, 36.

How do we explain the fact that, when confronted with the company of guards, Peter did not run? A coward certainly would have. Peter actually took out his sword and attacked the priest's servant. Peter went for the man's head, but the man evaded the stroke and Peter was only able to cut off the servant's ear. Peter's act was, without a doubt—bravado or not—an act of aggression. Soldiers and guards are trained to defend themselves and to fight back with deadly force when necessary. Any armed man in that company could have killed Peter without any problem. Peter must have also known that he was significantly outnumbered when he chose his course of action. We should not assume that Peter did not know or consider these possibilities. Otherwise, he would not have pulled his sword. And in spite of the danger, he did not shy away from the fight.

If anything, Peter's act can be described as foolish, done by an impulsive man against odds he could not overcome. *Cowardly* is the wrong description of Peter's character, yet this is precisely Boyd's choice. Jesus could not have known that the guards would not have killed Peter after the arrest based on Peter's character. After all, Peter had attacked the guards and they were entitled to respond with the same force Peter used. If the guards had killed or arrested Peter and put him away for the evening, he would not have been present at the courtyard to deny Jesus. If Peter had been killed or arrested, a later explanation that Jesus only meant that the prophecy would be fulfilled *if* Peter had made it to the campfire would not have been very convincing.

The implication that Peter's character flaw was cowardice does not hold water in light of what we know about the impulsive and aggressive nature of the disciple. The angry guards who came to arrest Jesus were not there to please Peter or to make sure that Jesus's prophecy was fulfilled. The God of the open view could not have known that Peter would survive the evening after he attacked the servant of the high priest. He could not have known that Peter would have the guts to show up at the campfire. Peter's courage was demonstrated under fire, and Jesus knew it. Even if we assume that Boyd's perspective on Peter's character is correct, this fact alone cannot explain how the God of open theism could have any assurances that Peter would deny Jesus *three times before the rooster crowed*!

Who was keeping track of the questions to make sure they were asked before the rooster crowed, especially since the people asking them were also free moral agents? (Regardless of whether the passage is speaking of an actual rooster or a sentinel that announced the time in the middle of the night, it does not matter.) How does Peter's character flaw influence the timing of the rooster's crowing? How did Jesus know that all the questions would be asked before such a time based on Peter's character flaw? What would have happened if one of the questioners had delayed his question until after the rooster crowed?

Here is the bottom line: *three free moral agents picked Peter out of the crowd without knowing about Jesus's prophecy.* The rooster certainly did not know about the prophecy. What could have motivated these three people to confront Peter while the illegal trial was going on? They couldn't have cared less who was around the campfire. They themselves were there by *accident*. That is, they were probably called to duty because of the unusual circumstances of the arrest. Jesus's prediction could not have been made if God had not known all of these details surrounding this event. Boyd states, "We do not need to believe that the future is exhaustively settled in God's mind to make sense of Jesus's prediction of Peter's denials."[124] I disagree. There is no possible way for the God of the open view to make this prediction without having exhaustive knowledge of the contingencies related to the events that led to the denials, to include the human players.

The God of open theism had no assurances that Peter would repent after the first denial or after the second. If the God of the open view made this prediction without knowing the details associated with it, he took a gigantic risk that could have turned Jesus into a liar just before his crucifixion. If any of the necessary circumstances had not led to exactly three denials, if any of the denials had taken place after the rooster crowed, if Peter had left the courtyard before the fulfillment of the prophecy, or if one of the questioners had not shown up, Jesus would have been declared a false prophet. How did the God of open theism know that the three questioners would come to the courtyard solely based on Peter's character?

---

[124] Boyd, 130.

Finally, we cannot ignore that the man whose ear was cut off had a family member present in the courtyard (Jn. 18:26). That fact could have been reason enough for Peter to stay away, but he followed Jesus in spite of the danger and possible fears. People can experience fear under certain circumstances without necessarily being cowards. This is especially true during war. Most soldiers experience the fears associated with battle, but they are not cowards. They get the mission done in spite of their fears and the imminent threat of death. Was Peter afraid? That's possible. Everyone entering a battlefield will experience fear. Was he a coward? The evidence does not support that conclusion. Peter's flaw was self-reliance, and he was about to learn a lesson in trusting God for his spiritual and physical strength that he would never forget. His self-reliance was exposed in public to create in him a spirit of humility to be the man Jesus needed him to be.

Peter's Lesson

Contrary to Boyd's assertions, Jesus's prediction of Peter's denial is a devastating blow to open theism. This is the reason Boyd jumps to Peter's restoration before considering the necessary details that led to the fulfillment of the prophecy. The fulfillment of this prediction was highly unlikely precisely because it ran counter to everything Jesus and the rest of the disciples knew about Peter. That is, of all the disciples, Peter was the least likely candidate to deny Jesus. Jesus did not predict Peter's denial because he knew Peter was a coward. On the contrary, Jesus predicted Peter's denial because *Peter's courage and self-reliance were well established facts and were a hindrance to his dependency on God by faith.* When Peter was restored, Jesus told him,

> I tell you the truth, when you were younger you dressed yourself and went where you wanted; but when you are old you will stretch out your hands, *and someone else will dress you and lead you* where you do not want to go. (Jn. 21:18, emphasis added)

Jesus knew of Peter's tendency to be self-sufficient. As a young man, Peter did whatever he wanted, but as an old man he would do what God wanted him to do. Peter would learn to depend on God even to the point of suffering the same death as Jesus. Peter had relied on himself for too long, and Jesus was going to change that to turn the disciple into a man of faith.

The moment a prediction involves the unpredictability of future human behavior, the character flaw argument falls apart. Even the least-ingrained character flaw on any of the other characters could have thwarted God's best laid plans. As Boyd has assured us repeatedly, too many people have frustrated God's will in the past. If Boyd actually believes that "we find God being frustrated as people stubbornly resist his plans," then he cannot use Jesus's desire to restore Peter as the solution to this self-created dilemma.[125]

Peter could just have stayed home, and Jesus's prediction would have become one more event that frustrated God. The facts demonstrate a different reality. Jesus made an absolute prediction, and the prophecy came through exactly as Jesus had predicted. There is not enough rationalization that can change the complexity of the prophecy. God foreknew the circumstances that would make Peter's denial a reality, and he made this fact known to his Son.

Conclusion

Let me share a few final thoughts on this event. First, Jesus's prediction was extraordinary precisely because of its unlikely fulfillment. That is, it was out of character for Peter to deny Jesus. Peter's aggressive act against a group of ruffians, including guards and soldiers, could be considered foolish, as a matter of military strategy, but not cowardly. Second, and more importantly, God could not have made such a prediction for that specific night unless he knew the events would unfold exactly as predicted.

Finally, the fact that God knew Peter's character perfectly did not eliminate the possibility that an unforeseen surprise could mess up the entire plan. What Jesus actually said, without conditions or hesitation, was, "Truly, I tell you, this very night, before the rooster crows, you will deny me three times." (Matt. 26:34 ESV). This was a prediction that could only come true if God knew, without a doubt, that all the events leading to Peter's denials would in fact take place. There

---

[125] Boyd, 62.

is, simply, no way for Jesus to predict all the events that surrounded Peter's denials solely based on Peter's character. Not Possible. I conclude this chapter with a quote from A. W. Tozer.

> Let us beware lest we in our pride accept the erroneous notion that idolatry consists only in kneeling before the visible objects of adoration, and that civilized peoples are therefore free from it. The essence of idolatry is the entertainment of thoughts about God that are unworthy of Him. It begins in the mind and may be present where no overt act of worship has taken place....
>
> Perverted notions about God soon rot the religion in which they appear. The long career of Israel demonstrates this clearly enough, and the history of the Church confirms it. So necessary to the Church is a lofty concept of God that when that concept in any measure declines, the Church with her worship and her moral standards declines along with it. The first step down for any church is taken when it surrenders its high opinion of God.[126]

---

[126] Bruce Ware, *Their God Is Too Small*, 128. [Quoted from A. W. Tozer, *The Knowledge of the Holy* (New York: Harper & Row, 1961)].

Do your best to present yourself to God as one approved, a workman who does not need to be ashamed and who correctly handles the word of truth.

—2 Timothy 2:15

Chapter FOUR
Trouble Passages

"The building has stairs that lead to nowhere, pillars that hang from the ceiling without purpose, and angled surfaces to create a sense of vertigo."[127] The purpose of the building was "to reflect life itself—senseless and incoherent. Upon hearing the explanation, Zacharias asked the guide one question, 'Did the architect do the same thing with the foundation?'"[128]

Apparently, the irony that the building was designed with a solid foundation, as opposed to a senseless and incoherent one, escaped the architect. The building was a monument dedicated to reject absolute truths as the foundation for a functioning society. But the building itself had a solid foundation that argued against the architect's intent.

The purpose of biblical hermeneutics is to accurately interpret God's revealed Word within their original context so that God's revealed character becomes comprehensible to the biblical student.

---

[127] Ravi Zacharias, *Can Man Live Without God?* (Nashville, TN: Thomas Nelson, 1994), 21.
[128] Ibid.

Additionally, biblical hermeneutics is an attempt to discover the truth to the researcher's best ability as others in the field challenge his conclusions and presuppositions. This exercise sharpens the researcher's own discoveries and brings greater clarity to the issues discussed.

Boyd has stated that his critics have not addressed the biblical evidence supporting open theism.[129] We will address the pertinent passages in order. We will review Romans 9, Ephesians 2, and Isaiah 46 and 48. Boyd presented a limited discussion on these passages in pages 29–32 of *The God of the Possible*. We will also take a look at the open view's tendency to cavalierly dismiss any supporting evidence of foreknowledge and to explain away more traditional interpretations.

Hermeneutics is the key issue in our discussion. Open theists also recognize the centrality of this issue since their approach to God's foreknowledge is based on a particular set of interpretative principles. Open theists have challenged the orthodox definitions of God, and a response is necessary. They have argued that the church has relied heavily on Greek philosophy to develop biblical doctrines. We need to point out that open theism has also relied on Greek philosophy to formulate the challenge to God's foreknowledge, as we discussed earlier.

Open Theism's Hermeneutical Parameters

The hermeneutical parameters of the open view are defined through the a priori presuppositions contained in their theological perspective. This is illustrated through phrases like "nescient principle," discussed by Lorenzo McCabe,[130] "exhaustively settled future,"[131] the "temporal-ness of God,"[132] "God's present knowledge,"[133] "the motif of future determinism,"[134] and "the Book of known facts" (this is a metaphor to illustrate the point that the future cannot be already written

---

[129] Boyd, 12.
[130] McCabe, *Divine Nescience of Future Contingencies*, 8.
[131] Boyd, 22.
[132] Hasker, "The Incompatibility of Libertarian Free Will and Divine Timelessness."
[133] Basinger, 163.
[134] Boyd, 13.

in some book).[135] These phrases have the intent of putting the classical view in a theological straitjacket to limit their argument options. Additionally, open theists want to redefine the debate as a struggle between a limited and dictatorial God (classical theology) versus an open-minded and generous God (openness theology).

Open theism's hermeneutical parameters can be summarized as follows: (1) Foreknowledge is incompatible with freewill. (2) Foreknowledge is a divine character flaw because it puts into question God's true motives in his so-called obsession to control people. (3) Foreknowledge makes God complicit with evil because he foreknows evil and still allows it to happen. (4) Foreknowledge makes God complicit with human sins as evidenced by Hitler's Holocaust. (5) Foreknowledge hinders God from holding people accountable for their actions because we are not truly free. (6) Foreknowledge makes God a deceiver because he has to create an illusion of freedom in order to make us feel accountable. (7) Foreknowledge makes God a hypocrite for wanting to save people whom he purposely created to be lost. These parameters are a summary of open theism's logical conclusions in their reaction to classical theology or theological determinism. While I agree with most of the criticism against theological determinism (Calvinism), I disagree that foreknowledge is equivalent to determinism, as we have amply demonstrated.

Limited Predestination Within the Open View

Open theists make a simple mistake from the outset in their understanding of God's character. For instance, Boyd has stated that "the future does not exist and cannot be known."[136] He has further said that "the future is settled to the extent that he [God] is going to determine it."[137] As a matter of hermeneutics and logic, these two statements cannot be true at the same time. If we take them to their logical conclusion, Boyd is advocating that God cannot know the future because the future does not exist while at the same time believing that God can be certain of the future if he determines it. If the future can be

---

[135] Boyd, 121–122.
[136] Ibid, 11.
[137] Ibid, 30.

certain when God determines it, then the future exists even if it only does in God's mind as exhaustive information. Either that or God is able to know something he does not know. Or, said another way, if God cannot know any part of people's future because people do not yet exist in the future, then God can never foreknow or predestine anything that relates to future human activity.

One of the biggest hermeneutical problems for open theists is their insistence of referring to the future as a concrete reality. Boyd states that if God knows the future, then people are not free to change their own futures. Our argument here is that God's knowledge of the future is neither causative nor based on God's preordination of human events. God's exhaustive information regarding future human events is based on his eternality and timelessness. God knows the entirety of the time-space continuum while allowing human history to progress in a linear fashion. Thus, future human choices cannot be changed, but not because God has fixed them. Rather, those decisions cannot be changed in the present time because those are the decisions people will freely make when their futures become their present. The best that can be said about the future from humanity's perspective is that people will never experience it as such. Therefore, the future is never a concrete reality for people, and we can never have the option of changing our futures.

God is different. His thoughts are higher than our thoughts. He can, and does, know the consequences of every decision every person makes every single second. He not only knows the decisions I make but the decisions every other person connected with me makes. God's knowledge of these continuous strings of decisions is as real to him as the present is to us. He is not dealing with possibilities. Rather, he knows how every decision made by every single person sets a course of action for every person. He can then intervene at key decision points to influence people's faiths and life directions. God knows these strings of decisions with absolute certainty, and he can project himself all the way to the end of time. He, therefore, knows the circumstances that will influence my decisions with such precision that he knows my future with absolute certainty. This is one way that God can intervene in human affairs without violating freewill. He has not restricted his foreknowledge. He has simply chosen to restrain his *meddling* in every little detail of human events. We suggest here that God only meddles in events related to his salvation plan and in answers to prayers when these are aligned with his plans.

God does not experience the future concretely for two reasons. First, God is Spirit. As such, God's only physical experience took place through Jesus's life during the thirty-plus years he lived among us. Second, the human future can be known only in the form of abstract information. God's knowledge of the future is directly related to his existence outside the span of universal history. He chooses to intervene at the appropriate times to influence the course of history without becoming the direct causal agent for human decisions or events.

For instance, the apostle Paul said that we "have been raised with Christ" and need to set our sights on the things of heaven (Col. 3:1). Paul was not saying that each Christian has been historically and physically raised with Christ. He was saying, however, that God knows with absolute certainty that believers have already taken the first step that will lead irrevocably to our resurrection with Christ. Accepting Christ as Savior is the first decision that unleashes a chain of events in which God enters into a reciprocal relationship with the believer that culminates with our resurrection during the rapture.

Similarly, Paul told the Philippians, "And I am sure of this, that he who began a good work in you will bring it to completion at the day of Jesus Christ" (Phil. 1:6). Thus, as far as God is concerned, we have been raised with Christ already. And that's exactly what is going to happen because our faith in Christ unleashed the chain of events in which the Holy Spirit will complete the work begun in us.

The apostle then encouraged believers to live in a way that is congruent with Jesus's resurrection. Paul's message is that God knows and sees us as already risen from the dead not because we are physically in heaven but because he has already seen our futures and can assure us of the blessing to be called his children. Whatever God knows, he knows ii as present reality because God does experience time. All human knowledge is always present knowledge. I cannot know today something that I will learn tomorrow. If I know anything, then, it is present knowledge. This is the reason that the word *foreknowledge* has meaning only for temporal creatures. From our perspective, God has foreknowledge. From his perspective, he simply knows the end from the beginning.

God's knowledge covers the entire spectrum of human history. He does not have a future per se. Only created beings, with a beginning and an ending, can have a future as an aspect of their existence that is not yet realized. Created beings are confined to a linear experience of time. This is so much so that we measure our lives through the consecutive measuring of time. The eternal God does not have any part of his existence that is yet to be formed or informed. He has knowledge. Both words, *future* and *foreknowledge*, have meaning only from the temporal linear existence of the creature. God is the eternal I AM THAT I AM (Ex. 3:14) that "makes the [human] future known" (Is. 48:3–6). Let us turn to some of the troubling passages in Boyd's work.

God's Intentions—Isaiah 46

Boyd's discussion of Isaiah 46 fails to address the most important open view premise—that God cannot know people's future. Boyd states, "[God] foreknows that certain things are going to take place because he knows *his own purpose and intention* to bring these events about."[138] If this assertion is correct, that God only knows the future to the extent that he has purposed and intends it, then not a single aspect of the discussion about people's future has any meaning. The issue has never been whether God can determine his own actions and bring them to fruition. There is no question God is able to design his own plans. The fact that God created the universe without human help should be strong enough evidence of God's ability to think for himself. He purposed to create, and he created.

To say that God has "exhaustively settled" his own plans is a meaningless word exercise couched in scholarship. Of course, God can exhaustively settle anything he wants regarding his plans. However, the God of open theism cannot be involved in settling anything in the future, exhaustively or otherwise, as it relates to people. The reader must remember that the God of open theism cannot know people's futures because they do not exist to be known. This is what open theists believe.

---

[138] Boyd, 30.

However, the God of the Bible is intimately involved in human affairs. Therefore, the internal cognitive processes of the God of the Bible cannot be divorced from his knowledge of people's choices and events. Otherwise, he would not be able to promise future blessings to people who have not yet been born. God's purposes in relationship to humans will stand because he knows how the historical events will unfold. Since, according to open theism, events in the human future are unknowable, we have to conclude that whatever the God of open theism purposes and intends about the future cannot include any human event.

Boyd interprets Isaiah 46 in an extremely narrow way. He suggests that God's purview regarding the future is only connected to what God has intended about himself, with the exclusion of any human involvement. Let me ask another question. Why should people care about God's intended purpose if it has no correlation to the human experience? We might as well be talking about aliens from outer space. If open theists are correct, then God's unlimited knowledge regarding his own choices is inconsequential to the human narrative. We would have to believe that God is making decisions regarding people's futures independent of any choices that they may actually make.

Additionally, if open theism is correct, then the God of open theism is more tyrannical than the God of foreknowledge. The God of open theism must establish the future in a historical and relational vacuum, which requires control and manipulation of people in the present in order to achieve his future purposes. As a general rule, people have no clue as to what God is thinking, much less what he knows regarding people's futures. Isaiah declared as much when he said,

> "For my thoughts are not your thoughts, neither are your ways my ways," declares the LORD. "As the heavens are higher than the earth, so are my ways higher than your way and my thoughts than your thoughts" (Is. 55:8–9)

There are two plausible ways that God can settle future events. First, he can do so because he has exhaustive noncausal information of human decisions and settle them in his mind but not in historical reality. Those events will happen as God knows them, but not because he becomes the primary cause of them. Or second, God can be unaware of the future but chooses to settle it in the form of blind predestination. An orthodox interpretation of God's omniscience has no problems accepting the first option, as we have discussed already. Open theists must accept the second option. Boyd said as much when he stated, "God can predestine and foreknows as settled whatever he sees fit to predestine and foreknow as settled."[139] According to Boyd, the God of open theism can predestine and foreknow a future that does not exist and cannot be known. I must confess that this is one of the most imaginative theological contradictions I have ever heard.

The reader needs to note that the second option only applies to people who are already living. That is, God's decision making is restricted to what exists now. Openness theology has stated that the God of the open view does not know people's futures, and he has no mechanism to determine who will be born in one hundred years. There is not enough material to manipulate in the present that can ensure that the God of open theism's desired ends will come to pass a hundred years in the future. This is a major problem for open theists. How can God's purposes stand if the God of open theism is unable to know what people will do tomorrow? Leading and directing history is outside the purview of the God of open theism. In an effort to defend the absoluteness of human freewill, open theism has actually destroyed the one mechanism by which it can be ensured—God's foreknowledge.

An Alternative Reading of Isaiah 46:1–11

Boyd quoted two passages out of Isaiah that point toward God's foreknowledge. He stated that these passages represent the strongest evidence for foreknowledge. The reality is that any and all prophetic passages must be understood as being very strong evidence in support of foreknowledge. These passages in Isaiah are not stronger or weaker evidence than any other prophetic revelation. However, since Boyd highlights these passages, let us address them in order. First, Isaiah stated,

> Remember the former things, those of long ago; I am God, and there is no other; I am God, and there is none like me. I make known the end from the beginning, from ancient times, what is

---

[139] Boyd, 53.

> still to come. I say, "My purpose will stand, and I will do all that
> I please." (Is. 46:9–10)

Boyd interprets God's foreknowledge as being limited to what God has purposed.[140] He stated that, when taken in context, the phrase "I make known the end from the beginning" does not imply a settled future. In other words, Boyd affirms his belief that God's claims to know the totality of human history, including the end, does not mean that God actually knows the totality of human history, including the end. He again employed the "partly settled future" concept in order to confuse the discussion. The *settledness* of the future is specifically connected to God's knowledge of the string of human decisions that will lead to specific results.

Since Boyd has defined the concept of the "partly settled future" in the narrowest of terms, he affirms that God has not preordained every human event in historical fact. We have argued that the settledness of the future is in the form of exhaustive, noncausative information. Therefore, God "declares the end from the beginning" because he has exhaustive, noncausal information of the totality of human history and not because he *causes* human history to happen or because his information regarding the future has already materialized in human history.

Once again, Boyd limits his discussion to the settled future concept because it brings us back to the straw man of determinism. That is, he has already implied that a settled future makes God the causal agent for all human behavior and responsible for evil. This is an error but a necessary technicality without which open theism cannot have a chance of standing.

Technically, Boyd is right when he says that the passage does not require a deterministic conclusion. I agree with him here, with a caveat. Since I do not hold that the biblical God is deterministic in his relationship to people, to argue against determinism where none exists is to put up a smoke screen. Therefore, while we agree that this passage does not require a deterministic conclusion, we are not in agreement as to why. God is not "declaring" that he has preordained every human event. The prophet is declaring that God "makes known the end from

---

[140] Boyd, 29–30.

the beginning," not that God has preordained it. God can declare the end from the beginning because of his exhaustive, noncausative knowledge of the totality of the human experience. The deterministic straw man requires that *foreknowledge* and *determinism* be interpreted as synonymous. This is a Calvinistic erroneous assumption that corrupts open theism's hermeneutical process.

Certainly, Boyd is entitled to interpret Isaiah 46 from the perspective of what God has purposed in his mind. However, this interpretation is unnecessarily restrictive. If we follow the passage to its conclusion, we find the following:

> Listen to me, you stubborn-hearted, you who are far from righteousness. I am bringing my righteousness near, it is not far away; and *my salvation* will not be delayed. I will grant salvation to Zion, my splendor to Israel. (Is. 46:12–13, emphasis added)

Boyd says, "The Lord is not appealing to information about the future he happens to possess; instead, he is appealing to his own intentions about the future."[141] This passage cannot be honestly interpreted exclusively in relationship to God's intentions. God is declaring his intentions to provide salvation to Zion (a reference to a human city in a specific geographical location), and he will not be deterred or discouraged from achieving his plan. We should note that God's "salvation" is a reference to Jesus. Luke said, "Blessed be the Lord God of Israel, for he has visited and redeemed his people and has raised up a horn of salvation for us in the house of his servant David" (Lk. 1:69). When Simeon saw Baby Jesus presented at the temple, he uttered these words: "Lord, now you are letting your servant depart in peace, according to your word; for my eyes have seen your salvation that you have prepared in the presence of all peoples" (Lk. 2:29–30).

The prophecy in Isaiah 46 was about the coming Messiah—God's salvation. While this was God's intent and purpose, he could not achieve this independently of human involvement. God had planned to use a young virgin as the vehicle to bring "his salvation" to Israel. Not only that, but God had to have known that Joseph would not reject Mary upon discovering that she was pregnant. It is clear that even in Jesus's case, God's intentions were not divorced from human involvement.

---

[141] Boyd, 30.

God's promises have never been made in a historical vacuum in which human agents are not involved. Whatever intentions God has had, they must always be interpreted with his relationship to humanity in mind.

That is, the Bible's main purpose is to reveal God's character to humanity in order to make our intimate relationship with him possible. This was true about Jesus in the flesh, but it is also true about Isaiah's prophecy. There is no logical or theological basis for God to reveal anything to people that is independent of his interaction with them. God's interventions in human affairs are always defined through people and never independent of them. I would like to hear any biblical prophecy, passage, or historical narrative in which God revealed anything that was irrelevant to God's relationship with humanity. Boyd's suggestion here is fatally flawed because God's purposes cannot be just a reference to what God has decided for himself. His purposes and intentions are always in reference to people. We are his only audience.

In order to accept the possibility of an exhaustively settled future concept in which God accomplishes his purposes without knowing people's futures, we would need to ignore the required element in God's plan of salvation—human faith—but this we cannot do. God's salvation is an act of grace, but faith is the required human response. The apostle Paul declared that faith comes by hearing and hearing by the word of God (Rom. 10:17). Faith is a gift of God in that every person born has received "a measure of faith" (Rom. 12:3). I believe Paul's intent was to reveal to us that the human capacity to believe is as innate to us as our ability to blink or breathe. Paul added that "salvation is by grace through faith" (Eph. 2:8). The following is a critical point. Faith, as the human response to the truth of the Gospel message, is never absent from the context of salvation because faith is the instrumental means through which God makes us alive.

Isaiah said the following regarding *how* God accomplishes his purposes. "From the east I summon a bird of prey; from a far-off land, *a man to fulfill my purpose*. What I have said, that will I bring about what I have planned, that will I do" (Is. 46:11). The phrase "a bird of prey" appears to be a reference to some form of judgment, or vessel of judgment. This probably could only be possible through the intervention of some foreign power. Regardless of how this judgment is interpreted, it will be achieved through a human vehicle. The God of open theism cannot make this prediction. God's promise in the passage is that in spite of the pending judgment, God will keep his promise to save Israel. The "bird of prey" is obviously a reference to a person (a king) or a kingdom. Both of these are distinctively human. Therefore, Isaiah is not saying that God will accomplish his purpose without human involvement. On the contrary, God *will* accomplish his purposes through the "bird of prey" that had not yet appeared in historical form. That is, the bird of prey is still in the future, and God is saying that he will bring this bird of prey "a man" to fulfill his purpose.

The prophet's message was that God was already at work to accomplish his purpose through human activity. This statement contradicts Boyd's assertion that Isaiah was simply revealing God's purpose about himself. The God of open theism cannot accomplish this incredible feat because he does not have any advanced information about the characters he has to call upon to bring about his purpose.

God's intentions are present in the passage, but God will achieve them through people. He will bring a *man* from "a far-off land" to fulfill his purpose. Who is this man that will fulfill God's purpose? How can the God of open theism be so confident that such a man will do as God intends? As stated earlier, the open view does not allow for God to know any uncreated future events. This must mean that the God of the open view cannot plan to fulfill his purpose through a yet unborn man, a man the God of open theism cannot know. This passage is devastating to the open view. It emphatically states that "God declares the end from the beginning" and that God will bring a man ("bird of prey") from "a far-off land" to do what God has foreknown he would do. The God of openness theology cannot count on a man who is yet to be born to accomplish anything.

The fact that God already knows that "a bird of prey" (a man) will fulfill his purpose in the distant future can only mean that, at the very minimum, God knows the identity of the bird of prey. Otherwise he could not make such a bold prediction. As Bible students, we have the advantage of hindsight. We can confirm whether the prophecy came through or not. This passage does not allow for Boyd's interpretation that the God of openness theology can make the promise to protect Israel solely based on his personal purposes. God must know the sociopolitical circumstances that made possible the appearance of the bird of prey. Additionally, God must know the human conditions that would bring the family of the bird of prey to the throne of his country. God cannot make this prediction solely based on what he wants without knowing the human conditions that would allow the prophecy's fulfillment.

God's Purpose Will Stand

Isaiah stated that God was "declaring the end from the beginning and from ancient times the things that are not yet done" (Is. 46:10 KJV). Boyd suggested that when we read the context properly, this passage does not speak of a God who has "exhaustively settled the future." I argue that the context of the passage cannot be explained if God's foreknowledge (God's ability to settle the future in his mind in the form of exhaustive, noncausative information) is taken out of the equation. Boyd stated that Isaiah 46:10 ESV—which reads in part, "My council shall stand, and I will fulfill my purpose"—establishes a conditional proposition that overrides the absolute statements of verses 9–11. Isaiah's statement in verse 11 is in the same context, but there is nothing in the context that requires a conditional interpretation of the passage. On the contrary, the statements in verses 9–10 appear to stand alone even within the context. That is, God's purpose will stand (his intentions) because he declares the end from the beginning. In other words, God is affirming the certainty of his purpose because he knows the future and not because he is ignorant of it.

It is crucial to understand Isaiah's purpose in this passage. God reveals his uniqueness, in relationship to other gods, within the context of his promises to Israel. The prophet differentiates God from idols in two ways. First, God is different from other gods in that he "makes known (*declares* ESV) the end from the beginning" (Is. 46:10). Please notice that Isaiah did not say "decreeing the end from the beginning." His specific statement is to reveal. Isaiah was making a contrast between God and idols, as we read in verse 9, "I am God, and there is none like me." According to Isaiah, the attribute that separates God from idols is that the God of Israel can reveal the future; thus, the phrase, "I make [the future] known." The only way God can make the future known is if he knows it. The God of Israel knows the future of his people, and he has revealed it to them.

This is not a minor issue. First, God is different from idols precisely because he knows the future and is able to make the future known to people through prophecy. He is the God that knows "from ancient times what is still to come" (Is. 46:10). Therefore, Israel can trust that God will sustain her through her gray hairs (Is. 46:4).

Second, God is different from other gods in that his "purposes will stand" (Is. 46:10). God's purpose in this context is his promise that he has sustained Israel "from ancient times" and will continue to sustain her (Is. 46:3–4). That is, God has worked on behalf of Israel's salvation "since you were conceived" (Is. 46:3–4). And in verse 4, we read that he promised to "sustain," to "carry," and "to rescue" Israel because he "made" her. There is no question that God's purpose within this passage is based on his promise to sustain Israel to old age (or until the end of this age). The people of Israel and the world can be sure that God's purpose will not be changed because he does as he pleases (Is. 46:10).

In order for God's future purpose for Israel to stand, God must work through people and not in spite of them. It is crucial to note that God will accomplish his purposes even working with a rebellious people. Or said if another way, Israel's disobedience will not be enough to thwart God's purposes. Thus, Isaiah 46:9–11 is not speaking out of both sides of the theological mouth. It can only be properly interpreted in light of God's election (past) and assured perseverance (future) of Israel, which is not possible without foreknowledge. God's promises will stand because he is not like idols that are mute. His promises withstand the passage of time. He is not shaping the future through coercion. He is navigating through human history, not working against it. God's greatness is affirmed when he works his purpose without violating human freewill.

Isaiah's main point, therefore, is to highlight the two fundamental qualities that make God distinct from all other gods—he makes the future known, and his promises will always stand. Boyd is free to say that God's revelation of the future is limited to what God has purposed for himself with the exception of human activity, but this passage does not support that interpretation. God's purpose in Isaiah 46 is not limited to what God has purposed about himself. Rather, it is a reference to how God is going to bring about the fulfillment of his promises to sustain Israel until the end, in spite of the judgment brought to Israel by the "bird of prey." God accomplishes his purpose through people, for people, and in people, and not in spite of them or independently of them.

Open Theism and God's Limited Knowledge

When we follow open theism's hermeneutics, we cannot avoid the conclusion that its proponents are repackaging McCabe's ancient nescient theory of God's knowledge. Boyd has said, "God exhibits a remarkable knowledge about the future of his chosen people."[142] The reader needs to remember that Boyd made this statement while maintaining that the future cannot be known because it does not exist. Mind you, Boyd does not say that God demonstrates *exhaustive knowledge* of his chosen people's future. He says that God "exhibits *remarkable* knowledge of their future." He speaks of God's knowledge of Israel's future as if it were some kind of lucky guess. This is like saying, "In spite of the fact that General Patton was an idiot, he exhibited remarkable combat and tactical expertise." It is clear that if people's futures do not exist to be known, then God cannot exhibit remarkable knowledge about anything in the nonexistent future.

We read further in *The God of the Possible*, "A number of times the Lord demonstrates foreknowledge of particular individuals and various events in their lives."[143] The inconsistent logic is simply staggering. In open view theology, God looks at the future and draws a blank, except when he chooses to foreknow particular individuals and events. This is maddening. How can God choose to know future individuals and events when they do not exist and are unknowable? Apparently, God's remarkable knowledge of individuals does not include the individuals' parents and grandparents. Does God know where this person will be born? Or does he just know the person without any context? Needless to say, it is very troubling that God can look into

---

[142] Boyd, 25.
[143] Ibid, 26.

people's futures and see only a broken and incomplete picture that has no relationship to the rest of reality.

Finally, Boyd implies that God has limited knowledge of even Jesus's life, saying, "Many passages of Scripture make clear that God foreknew and foreordained *aspects* of Christ's ministry, especially his death."[144] What kind of statement is that? If God foreordained only some aspects of Jesus's life, then there must have been some aspects of Jesus's life and ministry that God knew nothing about. Otherwise, why not foreordain Jesus's entire life? I cannot even conceive how a theologian can suggest that aspects of Jesus's life were not fully known to God. If there was a life on this earth that had every single aspect of his existence foreordained, Jesus had to be the one.

We can draw two preliminary conclusions. First, open theists equate foreknowledge with preordination. Preordination, by definition, is an *a priori* decision that places God on the side of "showing favoritism." We already know God cannot do such a thing because he has said as much (Acts 10:34). When Paul wrote to the Roman church that "for those whom he *foreknew* he also *predestined* to be conformed to the image of his Son, in order that he might be the firstborn among many brothers" (Rom. 8:29, emphasis added), he was not speaking about preordination.

Paul statement that foreknowledge *precedes* predestination was a reference to inevitable conclusion to the process those who were in Christ would experience. That is, those whom God foreknew would accept God's free gift of eternal life in Christ, will also "be conformed to the image of his Son." In this passage predetermination was not a reference to God selecting a group of individuals unto eternal life before the foundation of the world. Instead, predestination indicated that the logical conclusion of being in Christ resulted in conformity to the image of Christ. The predestination was not about salvation, but it was a predestination after salvation. Those who were saved, would be conformed to Christ.

We can ask, what was it that God foreknew? What was it that God knew ahead of time that allowed him to say with confidence that believers would be conformed? I will venture to say that God knew

---

[144] Boyd, 27.

ahead of time the men and women who, upon hearing the gospel, would believe and be made alive through faith. That is, God's foreknowledge is not based on a pre-established reality. Instead, it appears that God settled the future based on his foreknowledge of the future and not the other way around.

God Has Foretold the Future
Isaiah 48:3–6

Let us take a look.

I *foretold* the former things long ago, my mouth announced them, and I made them known; then suddenly I acted, and they came to pass. For I knew how stubborn you were; the sinews of your neck were iron, your forehead was bronze. Therefore, I told you these things long ago; before they happened, I announced them to you so that you could not say, "My idols did them; my wooden image and metal god ordained them." You have heard these things; look at them all. Will you not admit them? From now on I will tell you of new things, of hidden things unknown to you. (Is. 48:3–6)

Boyd interpreted this passage thus: "In other words, as a supernatural means of confronting the lie that idols have power to bring about events, Yahweh announced and then manifested *his sovereign ability* to bring about events." He then added, "This is not simply a matter of the Lord possessing information about what was going to take place. It was rather a matter of the Lord *determining* what was going to take place."[145] Very few people would reject the idea that God can do whatever he pleases. God's power is not the issue in this discussion and never has been. The issue is whether the God of the open view can determine a future event that includes people he does not know would exist to accomplish a purpose that does not yet exist for those people.

The only way that God can foretell the future is if he knows it. Only the classical view of God's foreknowledge affords to God the ability to make the future known. God revealed to Isaiah that his

---

[145] Boyd, 31.

attribute to "make [the future] known" separates him from idols. It is precisely this quality that makes God different from and superior to idols, and not, as Boyd contends, God's ability to bring about events. You don't have to be God to bring about events. People bring about events all the time. Isaiah's point is that only the God of Israel can make the future known. His point was *not* that God could determine the future. Determining the future is not exclusive to God. People can set circumstances in the present that can determine short-term future events. For instance, I can determine my own future when I say, "I will be playing golf tomorrow at ten in the morning." If I am alive tomorrow and in good health, I will be playing golf tomorrow. I just determined my future, with the caveat that I really do not know as a matter of fact that I can actually make it to the golf course.

God's knowledge of the future is in a different category. My knowledge of the future is nothing more than a plan or a wish. My plans to play golf can never be described as predetermined, mostly because I really do not know the future. For instance, I will fulfill my purpose if I am alive, if my children are safe, and if it does not rain. In other words, since I do not control those conditions, I don't *know* if I will play golf tomorrow. God knows the future with certainty because he also knows all the variables that will influence the unfolding events.

Boyd goes on to say, "The verse doesn't support the view that the future is exhaustively settled *in reality* and thus exhaustively settled in God's mind" [emphasis added].[146] Again, Boyd sets up a straw man and then argues against a concept that nobody is advancing. Only theological determinists argue that God has settled the future in *reality*. Boyd is fighting against this error, but he makes his own error by defining foreknowledge using the deterministic terms. Let us not be taken by this deceitful declaration. Open theists have argued that God cannot exhaustively know the future, and thus the future cannot be settled in God's mind *because it has not yet become a historical reality*. This is nonsense. Information does not have to be settled in concrete reality in order to be legitimate information. The settled-ness of the future does not depend on the reality of the events. Instead, it depends on the reliability of the information God *knows ahead of time regarding*

---

[146] Boyd, 31.

the decisions that people will freely make, and he alone has the purview to know those decisions.

Any knowledge that God has of the future is not in the form of concrete historical reality because people have not lived their futures. God's knowledge of the future is conceptual. That is, as stated earlier, he has exhaustive, noncausal information about the events that have not yet happened. This is the point of foreknowledge—it is having exhaustive information ahead of time about things that have not yet happened. Since life experiences are irrevocably tied to the present, it is incongruent to speak of the future as "settled in reality." Therefore, people's futures can never be settled in historical reality because it has not yet occurred. But it would be a stretch of gargantuan proportions to extrapolate that God's mind is not able to anticipate people's future. Please read carefully the quote again.

> The verse doesn't support the view that the future is exhaustively settled *in reality,* and thus exhaustively settled in God's mind.

The first clause of the statement is curious. Boyd states that God has not settled the future in concrete reality, but we are not making this argument. We agree that the future does not exist in concrete reality. What we are arguing here is that the future exists in God's mind in the form of exhaustive, noncausal information. If he has exhaustive information about the future, he can make it known. If God does not have exhaustive information about the future, then it follows that he cannot make the future known—or partly settle it, as Boyd argues. Either God has exhaustive information about the future, or he does not. The perfect God, Creator of the universe, cannot partly know.

Boyd's expectation is that the initial reaction by the readers will be something like this: "Of course the future cannot be settled in reality if that reality has not happened." But the straw man does not stand up to close scrutiny. It is an error to equate human concrete reality with God's abstract spiritual reality. The suggestion is that God's mind is limited to understanding the whole of reality from the perspective of concrete human events. Nothing could be further from the truth.

Let us see what happens if we invert the original sentence. The inverted quote reads, "The verse does not support that the future is exhaustively settled in God's mind and thus is not exhaustively settled in reality." The argument that a settled event in God's mind translates into a settled human event in reality is a non sequitur. The first problem with the inverted order is that the text *does* support the idea that the future is settled in God's mind. Additionally, Boyd's logic breaks down further because it is very possible to believe that future human events could be settled in God's mind without necessarily being settled in human reality. Since the original statement is based on the presupposition that nothing outside of known *concrete* reality exists, then God's ability to settle the future in his own mind must be subordinated *to what is settled in human reality*. However, since *it is possible* that something could be settled in God's mind before becoming part of human reality, then Boyd's carefully crafted statement is patently false.

There is another problem with the hermeneutics of open theism regarding Isaiah 48:3–6. Open view theologians cannot truly believe that God is able to predetermine future human events without knowing the historical context in which those events will unfold. What is Boyd referring to when he says that God can predetermine some of the events that are going to take place? He cannot be saying that God will force people, at the appropriate time, to conform to a preordained result. If that was Boyd's intent, then that would be a contradiction to his carefully crafted absolute libertarian freewill idea.

Boyd's logic is flawed for the following reasons. First, God cannot preordain future human behavior without knowing the future circumstances surrounding of the preordained behavior. Similarly, God cannot preordain future behavior without knowing whether the people responsible to perform the preordained behavior will be born at all. Second, since future human behavior does not exist to be known and neither do the people themselves, the God of open theism cannot predetermine future human events without knowing whether the people involved in the events will actually be born. How can the God of open theism predestine something without knowing the place and the possible political, cultural, and religious contexts of the time in which the event will take place? He cannot do such a thing. Boyd has already established that prophecies are conditional, thus negating the possibility that the God of open theism can truly predetermine any future human events.

Third, we cannot reasonably expect, within open theism's theory, that people yet unborn will perform the tasks God has predetermined without rebelling against God. The problem here is that Boyd has already established that people rebel against God constantly and God has been impotent to prevent them from doing so. Therefore, God really cannot count on people to do anything for him.

And finally, in order for Boyd's position to be true, we have to accept that God's foreknowledge of the future is not real because it is not connected to historical facts. Not once open theists address the issue of noncausative information. In their system, the God of open theism is constrained in his knowledge of the future because he is dependent on people's creative actions to acquire knowledge based on reality. These four contradictions make the open view's logic incomprehensible.

Two New Testament Examples

Boyd's hermeneutics are on more solid ground when he discusses the relationship between God's grace and humanity's freewill. His discussions of Ephesians 2 and Romans 9 are very consistent with the classical Arminian view of freewill. I agree that both passages give greater emphasis to humanity's role in appropriating salvation than the deterministic view allows, but I must add that Boyd's discussion on these two passages do not support open theism. During his discussion of both passages, Boyd keeps trying to interject the open view as a sensible alternative to the deterministic view, but I do not find him effective in doing so. A more credible argument can be made for freewill within these two passages without imposing open view hermeneutics on them. Let's look at the passages one at a time.

Ephesians 2

Boyd's discussion of Ephesians 2:8–10 points out how the classical view deemphasizes humanity's obligation to appropriate

God's gracious gift. Let me summarize Boyd's three points in his discussion of Ephesians 2:8–10.[147]

First, he correctly points out that if people are not free to choose salvation, then God must be responsible for everyone's decisions. If God is responsible for people's choices, then all calls to repentance are irrelevant.

Second, he also correctly states that faith is not works. This is not a shocking revelation since this point is evidently clear in Paul's words. The apostle stated, "For it is by grace you have been saved, through faith—and this is not from yourselves, it is the gift of God—*not by works*, so that no one can boast" (Eph. 2:8–9). Paul clearly stated that faith and works are not comparable or interchangeable.

Third, Boyd proposes that the Holy Spirit's work is best understood as making "it *possible* for us to believe, but he does not make it *impossible not* to believe."[148] That is, the Holy Spirit enables people to exercise their faith, but he is not actively blocking us from believing or disbelieving. This appears to be an indictment on the irresistible grace argument within Calvinism, but it is a sensible approach to the role of the Holy Spirit in drawing people to faith in God.

I have an objection to this third point. I believe the Holy Spirit uses the truth revealed in the preaching of the gospel to awaken people's ability to faith. Faith is not an active element in the salvation process. Instead, we should understand faith as an instrumental means. That is, God uses the already existing "measure of faith" to channel his grace to make us alive. I do not believe the Holy Spirit's role is to level the playing field so that people can believe. My position is that the Holy Spirit activates life when people hear the truth of God's word. Thus, Paul stated that "faith comes by hearing, and hearing by the word of God."

With the objection, Boyd's three points are an acceptable interpretation of Ephesians 2. However, he doesn't address the issue at hand. In other words, his exposition on this passage does not advance the theory that God does not know the future or that the future does not

---

[147] Boyd, 137–138.
[148] Ibid, 138.

exist in God's mind in the form of exhaustive, noncausative information.

Why do these three previous points not advance the open view? Boyd effectively argues against the deterministic perspective with his three points. However, since we hold that the deterministic perspective is not an accurate description of God's character, as presented by Paul in Ephesians, to use this passage to argue against determinism and in favor of the open view is wrongheaded.

We need to add an additional comment in this section regarding Paul's description of humans being *dead in sin* (Eph. 2:1). Boyd asks the obvious question, "How can we even choose salvation, however, if we are *'dead' in sin*?"[149] The phrase "dead in sin" is more properly understood as an individual's inability to do good works that would lead to salvation. However, being "dead in sin" has never meant, to my knowledge, that humans are incapable of moral decision-making, that they are not responsible for their actions, or that they cannot hear the gospel and ascertain its truth.

Said in another way, unredeemed men and women are in a spiritual state of enmity against God, but they can still hear, receive, and respond to the gospel. Otherwise, the preaching of the gospel would be a waste of time. Men and women will remain in a state of rebellion against God until the Holy Spirit awakens their faith through the proclamation of God's Word. This means that when people hear the gospel, the Holy Spirit awakens their souls to their need of a Savior. The movement of the Holy Spirit is an integral part of preaching and hearing. Thus, the apostle Paul stated, "Faith comes by hearing and hearing by the word of God" (Rom. 10:17). The Holy Spirit can accomplish his purposes any way he wants, but the most common method is through the preaching of the gospel. This is the reason that preaching the gospel to the entire world is such an important command for the church. It is in the preaching of God's Word that humanity's faith is stirred in their souls and they are saved.

Allow me to make some observations about true salvation. First, the Holy Spirit brings people to the point of repentance through the preaching of the gospel. Second, Jesus performed the works of salvation

---

149 Boyd, 138.

on our behalf. Third, Jesus lived a righteous life and died for the sins of the world so that his life would be imputed to us and we would not have to die. Fourth, Jesus's blood cleanses people from sin, and his life is imputed as righteousness to those who accept God's gracious gift through faith. The following is a short summary of Jesus's works of salvation: he paid the penalty for sin with his life, he took God's wrath for humanity's sins upon himself, he was buried instead of us, he fulfilled the requirements of the law with his death (the law had imposed a death sentence against humanity and Jesus paid it, even though he was sinless—2 Cor. 5:21), and he gave humanity life when he rose from the dead.

Individuals cannot perform these works on their behalf. If people were left to pay for their sins, the result would be eternal damnation. God's justice demanded a penalty for sin, and he would be justified to sentence every person to eternal death, for "all have sinned and fall short of the glory of God" (Rom. 3:23). Thus, people cannot perform good works that lead to salvation.

Since faith is not works and since people retain their capacity to believe, the Holy Spirit stirs people's souls through the proclamation of the gospel to bring them to repentance. The proclamation of the gospel assumes that sinful people have the capacity to believe. For instance, we read in Mark's gospel that a woman suffering from an issue of blood "had heard the reports about Jesus and came up behind him in the crowd and touched his garment. For she said, 'If I touch even his garments, I will be made well'" (Mk. 5:27–28). The woman believed that Jesus could heal her because she had heard. That is, she was the one who heard, and she was the one who believed. In Luke, we read, "The shepherds returned, glorifying and praising God for all they *had heard* and seen, as it had been told them" (Lk. 2:20, emphasis added). The shepherds praised God because they had heard and seen the birth of God's Son.

We can cite many more instances in which faith was awakened in a person through hearing the gospel. But I will quote the apostle Paul, when he wrote,

> But what does it say? "The word is near you, in your mouth and
> in your heart" (that is, the word of faith that we proclaim);

> because, if you confess with your mouth that Jesus is Lord and believe in your heart that God raised him from the dead, you will be saved. For with the heart one believes and is justified, and with the mouth one confesses and is saved. (Rom. 10:8–10)

These passages appear to suggest that people can respond in faith to the hearing of the gospel message. This does not negate any role that the Holy Spirit plays in the proclamation of the gospel. However, Paul's implication is that "the word of faith we proclaim" is "near your heart." Paul is saying that faith is in the heart of people ready to respond upon hearing the gospel message.

Paul's words that we were "dead in trespasses and sin" (Eph. 2:1) have been misinterpreted to mean that people were incapable of exercising faith. I do not think Paul was saying anything like that. I believe Paul was saying that we were dead to God. That is, before hearing the gospel, we experienced life only from the perspective of the sinful nature that leads to death. Paul continued by saying that we were mixed up with the sons of disobedience, "among whom we all once lived in the passions of our flesh" (Eph. 2:3). Did you see it? On the one hand, Paul stated that we were "dead in trespasses and sin." On the other, he said that "we lived" among the sons of disobedience. This could only mean that while we were "dead in trespasses and sins" and thus unable to experience the life than comes from God's Spirit, we were sufficiently alive to experience the "passions of the flesh" and respond to the gospel.

Upon hearing the gospel, each person is able to come to a conscious decision to believe or not to believe. A person's decision to believe is freely made, but not without the convicting intervention of the Holy Spirit. Some within the classical view may hold that people are incapable of moral decision-making or even to exercise faith on their own. But believing the opposite—that humans are able to make free choices—is not an argument for the open view. In either case, our ability to believe is a statement about the God who made provisions for our reconciliation to Him.

Luke recorded for us Paul's encounter with King Agrippa (Acts 25:13–26:32). Allow me to share one more statement regarding that meeting. Paul told Agrippa that he "was not disobedient to God's calling" (Acts 26:19). This could only mean that Paul believed that Agrippa was being disobedient to the gospel message. This discussion is to say that faith is not works because it is a gift of God to every person as part of the package of being human. Our package includes all the five senses, our capacity for moral understanding and behavior, and our capacity to believe or to rebel against God.

God's grace is *sufficient* for salvation in that people are the beneficiaries of God's good heart to offer eternal life at no cost to us, even though it cost everything to him. Additionally, grace is *necessary* for salvation because God had to initiate and choose to offer us his unmerited gifts of eternal life. Boyd's attempt to make freewill contingent upon an open view interpretation of the future, as if there was a cause-and-effect correlation between the two, does not follow. We have already seen that there is no contradiction between God's foreknowledge and people's ability to make free moral decisions. Therefore, freewill and foreknowledge coexist in God's universe—even if open view theologians cannot grasp the mechanics that make it possible.

Romans 9

Romans 9 presents a more complicated challenge than the Ephesians passage does.[150] Again, Boyd made a fair assessment of the deterministic position as it relates to Romans 9. The deterministic position basically states that salvation and damnation are ultimately dependent on God's will without giving proper consideration to the role that faith and freewill play in the process. While this is a very common interpretation of this passage, it is by no means the only one. Historically, both the Arminian position on freewill and the Calvinistic position on God's sovereignty or deterministic position have been accepted as being within the bounds of orthodox theology. I need to clarify here that this book is not an exercise to discredit either the Calvinistic or Arminian theological systems. I accept both as plausible explanations to God's sovereignty and human freewill, even though I have strong reservations regarding both systems. But that is a subject

---

[150] Boyd, 139.

for a different day. The question here is about the hermeneutics of open theism and not about discrediting the historically orthodox theological systems. That said, let us take a closer look at Romans 9.

Salvation Belongs to God
Romans 9:14–16

In this passage, Paul described God's role in salvation without denying human responsibility. Paul wrote the following:

> What then shall we say? Is God unjust? Not at all! For he says to Moses, "I will have mercy on whom I have mercy and I will have compassion on whom, I have compassion." *It does not, therefore, depend on man's desire or effort, but on God's mercy.* (Rom. 9:14–16)

This passage has been interpreted to mean that God made the decision to save humanity from the consequences of sin independently of any human responsibility or accountability. While I do not pretend to know what God decided in eternity, this passage does not support that presupposition. I believe God decided in eternity past to create this system in such a way that he could extend his mercy to anyone who believed the message of the gospel. God's decision to save sinners was based on God's love. Thus, Paul says, "It does not depend on man … but on God's mercy." Or said another way, people do not get to choose the method, or the motivation God would use to redeem his creation. The apostle is not excluding the role faith plays in the salvation process. He is simply stating an eternal truth—God decided to save anyone who believes because of his mercy.

John said it this way: "For God so loved the world that he gave his one and only Son, that whoever believes in him shall not perish but have eternal life" (Jn. 3:16). God's love was demonstrated in the decision to save sinners. Jesus's life was the physical evidence of this love. And John said that people's faith ("Whoever believes will be saved") was an integral part of the process to *receive* eternal life. God's decision to save all who believe was made in eternity past and independently of people. Thus, God created humanity with a "measure or faith" that allows them to respond to the gospel and receive salvation. People are truly free to receive or reject God's invitation to be saved.

The personalization of Romans 9 has resulted in many of the interpretation errors associated with the passage. Personalization occurs when a general principle revealed in a passage of Scripture is applied to particular individuals. Many times, such passages are allegorical references to the entire human race as opposed to individuals. This appears to be the case regarding Romans 9. I believe Paul's reference to Esau and Jacob is intended to show God's compassion without prejudice. Theoretically, if Esau had not sold his birthright, he would have received Isaac's blessing. However, when God revealed to Rebekah that "the older would serve the younger" (Gen. 25:23), he was not taking a wild guess. He foreknew that Esau was going to be a vain and superficial man.

When Esau, in his vanity and pride, sold his birthright to Jacob for a bowl of soup, he proved his unworthiness to receive the blessing, and God's foreknowledge of Esau's character was affirmed. The point we are making here is that God foreknew Esau's sale of his birthright and his disregard for the blessing. God foreknew this sequence of events before the twins were born, and he made it known. God was not more specific (he did not specifically describe the selling of the birthright) to safeguard the boys' freewill. But God revealed enough information to the Rebekah to make clear that the blessing would not come through the firstborn. She did not know how did was going to happen, but God did, as he always does.

The God of the open view could not have predicted the reversal of roles for at least two reasons. First, the God of the open view could not have foreknown about Esau's selling of his birthright because Esau had not created the event, and Boyd has assured us that God only knows created events. Esau's selling of his birthright was a future event that the God of the open view could not know. Second, the God of the open view could not have foreknown how Rebekah and Jacob would manipulate Isaac to acquire the birthright.

God was merciful to Jacob for his faith but rejected Esau's cavalier attitude toward God's blessing. While the prophecy does not expand on Esau's character failures, there is little doubt that Esau demonstrated his unworthiness to be the precursor of the coming Messiah long before the bowl of soup incident. Both Rebekah and Jacob understood this aspect of Esau's character. The sale of the birthright was the culmination of a lifelong series of character misjudgments by Esau.

Thus, Paul recalls the statement "the older will serve the younger" because the apostle understood how God selected people for service (Rom. 9:12). Esau was a vain man unable to focus on spiritual things. God did not reject Esau in favor of Jacob because Jacob was a better man or because he was better looking. We all know that Jacob did not always behave in the most ethical manner, but he had a higher value about his father's inheritance in God's plan. God revealed the twins' future because he foreknew that Esau would fail to value his birthright blessing. He also knew that Jacob would want to acquire it from Esau. Jacob understood the far-reaching consequences of the blessing, while Esau did not.

God also foreknew the lengths to which Jacob was willing to go to receive the blessing—a testimony to his persistent faith. This was not a secret to God, even if it was a secret to Isaac. Paul stated that God's election is "not by works, but by him who calls" (Rom. 9:11). If salvation is by grace through faith, then Jacob received the blessing through faith, and Esau lost the blessing because of his lack of faith.

The most reasonable interpretation of Romans 9 is that God foreknew Jacob's faith, and that became the basis for his election—not any capricious decision by God. The prophecy to Isaac and Rebekah was not a blind guess. God had seen the totality of the twins' future and told their parents that the "older will serve the younger." Foreknowledge is the only way God could make this prediction. This is what foreknowledge is all about—God making the future known.

If you follow the twins' lives, it is apparent that they made their choices on their own. While this was going on, God sat back and watched as his prophecy was being fulfilled. God knew how both boys would respond to God's promised blessing as adults, as well as how the parents would handle the twins' feud. Since God does not show favoritism, it is not possible for their election to have been made based on blind prejudice (Rom. 2:11; Acts 10:38). Please understand, Paul was not talking about eternal salvation in this passage. He was, specifically, speaking about the blessing to be the coming Messiah's lineage. If we lose sight of this point, we will mangle the passage beyond recognition, which is what Calvinists have done.

The phrase "I will have compassion on whom I have compassion" is not evidence that God chooses individual persons in a faithless vacuum. I think this phrase implies two principles. First, people cannot dictate to God *how* he should exercise his compassion. This verse declares that God is free to determine the method he will use to exercise his compassion. Second, people cannot limit to *whom* God would show compassion. The text is not saying that God would have compassion on a preselected group. He is saying that he will not discriminate on whom he will have compassion. That's the reason God has declared that he will extend his compassion to "whosoever believes." In order to make salvation possible, God sent Jesus to serve as propitiation for us (Rom. 3:25; 1 Jn. 2:2). God decided that Jesus's sacrifice would satisfy his demand for justice for the sins of the entire world. Once God's justice was satisfied, he was free to have compassion on whom he has compassion.

Paul's intention in this passage was not to explain God's arbitrariness in salvation. On the contrary! Paul was emphasizing God's impartiality in his salvation process. The apostle's focus is on God's freedom to dispense his grace without playing favorites. God's choice to have compassion for mankind is nondiscriminatory, and this decision is not based on race, culture, birth order, or national origin. Luke quotes Peter in describing God's nondiscriminatory grace: "I now realize how true it is that God does not show favoritism but accepts men from every nation who fear him and do what is right" (Acts 10:34–35). Paul adds a similar sentiment in Ephesians 6:9 and Colossians 3:25. The apostle Paul also wrote,

> There will be trouble and distress for every human being who does evil: first for the Jew, then for the Gentile; but glory, honor and peace for everyone who does good: first for the Jew, then for the Gentile. *For God does not show favoritism.* (Rom. 2:9–11)

God's compassion is shown in his impartiality and not in his arbitrary choices. We cannot dictate to God to whom he will show mercy. Esau was the rightful heir according to humanity, but Jacob was the rightful heir according to God—based on faith. The fact that Esau was the firstborn was not the determining factor for God. Faith was the determining factor for God's election of Jacob over Esau. Esau was not a man of faith, but Jacob was.

What about Paul's statement regarding Jacob and Esau? Was Paul not referring to God's election of Jacob before the twins were born? Was not the election made regardless of their faith? Allow me to share the passage in question with you.

> Not only that, but Rebekah's children had one and the same father, our father Isaac. Yet, before the twins were born or had done anything good or bad—in order that God's purpose in election might stand: not by works but by him who calls—she was told, "The older will serve the younger." Just as it is written: "Jacob I loved, but Esau I hated." What then shall we say? Is God unjust? Not at all! For he says to Moses, "I will have mercy on whom I have mercy, and I will have compassion on whom I have compassion." (Rom. 9:10–15)

To interpret Paul's reference of the incident between Jacob and Esau as a divine capricious act without considering both men's expressions of faith is not consistent with Scripture. Paul's statement that Rebekah was told that "the older will serve the younger" is an indication of God's foreknowledge of the twins' characters and not an indication that God was playing favorites (Rom. 9:12). God knew "before the twins were born" that Esau would sell his firstborn rights for a bowl of soup. God foreknew that Jacob would be coached by Rebekah to place a higher value on their father's blessing than Esau. God foreknew that Esau would be a fool, and he also foreknew that Jacob would be more ambitious and faithful than his brother. And God knew all these facts before the twins were born. Let me add a statement as it relates to open theism. Regardless of how God made the election, the God of open theism could not have predicted that the older would serve the younger. Thus, Romans 9 does not help or advance open theism one bit.

Not one aspect in God's election process of the twins' lives was divorced from the human dynamics that created the environment for the twins' choices. Paul is affirming God's foreknowledge when he summarizes the twins' lives from God's perspective in election. To interpret God's election as being independent of Jacob's and Esau's faith, or lack thereof, is the error of the passage personalization. As the reader will notice, Paul returns to his faith theme in Romans 9:30–33, which is Paul's emphasis throughout the entire book of Romans. God's election of Jacob ("Jacob I loved") and his rejection of Esau ("Esau I hated"), were based on God's foreknowledge of the twins' faith response to God and not on God's stubborn and unjust bias of selecting one over the other.

Even though this passage is not primarily about people's role in salvation, Paul stated that God's salvation process includes men's faith response to the gospel. Therefore, the role played by faith cannot be easily dismissed. Read with me:

> What then shall we say? That the Gentiles, who did not pursue righteousness, have obtained it, *a righteousness that is by faith;* but Israel, who pursued a law of righteousness, has not attained it. Why not? *Because they pursued it not by faith but as if it were by works.* They stumbled over the "stumbling stone. (Rom. 9:30–32, emphasis added)

Esau represented the "Israel who pursued a law of righteousness," and Jacob represented the Gentiles who pursued a "righteousness that is by faith." Paul uses the allegory of Jacob and Esau to bring home the point of God's election of the Gentiles by faith. His reference to Esau and Jacob was not directly related to the twins. Rather, Paul used God's election of Jacob to be the Messiah's ancestor to illustrate God's election of the Gentiles, as a group and not as individuals. The issue in Romans 9, as it has been throughout this entire epistle, was God's expectation that after people had heard the gospel, they would respond with faith. The apostle Paul affirms the principle of election by faith in his letter to the Galatians' church: "The Scripture foresaw that God would justify the Gentiles by faith and announced the gospel in advance to Abraham: 'All nations will be blessed through you'" (Gal. 3:8).

Paul's point with the twins' allegory was to illustrate God's having mercy upon whom he has mercy—in this case, the Gentiles. I believe it's an error to interpret Romans 9 to mean that God elects individuals in an arbitrary manner and independent of responding to the gospel with faith. As the readers can see, God's election of Gentiles was not done independently of their faith response to the gospel. This is Paul's entire point—God saves based on his foreknowledge of people's future faith. God revealed Jacob's election based on his foreknowledge of his faith. There cannot be any other explanation if God is to remain impartial.

God culminated his salvation plan when Jesus, God's gracious gift to humanity, came to die for the sins of all. And he finishes his salvation purpose when people receive Jesus's sacrifice by faith. Paul declared that God's decision to save man was not based on his justice or on people's need for salvation, but on God's mercy. This means that the gift of salvation is God's merciful initiative toward humanity, and he has not, or will not, change his gracious gift based on human insecurities and frailties. Paul was not saying, at least not from my perspective, that God had pre-established a by-name salvation roster of the individuals who would be saved, or lost, independent of any faith in response to Christ's cross.

Therefore, salvation is always by grace (God is always the initiator of salvation) through faith (people are always required to respond to God's grace). If these two elements are distorted, God's salvation process cannot be properly understood (Eph. 2:1–10). God promised to save all who come to Jesus in faith, and he does.

Jeremiah, Paul, and the Potter

The prophet Jeremiah revealed God's foreknowledge when he stated, "Before I formed you in the womb I knew you" (Jer. 1:5). This passage is not a figure of speech. That is, God revealed to the prophet that he had specific information regarding the kind of man Jeremiah would be. God knew this information before Jeremiah was formed in his mother's womb. God appointed him as a prophet to the nations before Jeremiah had thought of uttering a word. God knew that Jeremiah would be a man of faith who would stand for God regardless of the circumstances. And do you know what happened? Jeremiah became the man God had foreknown he would become. Please understand that God's knowledge was not tied to the physical reality of Jeremiah's conception. God knew Jeremiah *before* he was formed in his mother's womb.

That is, before Jeremiah was physically conceived, God already had a picture of Jeremiah's character as a man. The God of the open view cannot make this statement. The God of the open view could not have appointed Jeremiah as a prophet to the nations before his birth because the historical event of Jeremiah's birth was not known until after it happened. Regarding this passage, Boyd must believe that Jeremiah exaggerated God's role in his calling by making the assertion that God had appointed him before his birth. Or, worse, Boyd believes that the passage is not an authentic revelation of God.

This is a significant indication that the God of the Bible can reveal that he knew a person, Jeremiah, before that person's birth. This is an important issue. Either this passage is a true statement regarding what God knew about Jeremiah, or it is not. If God knew Jeremiah before his conception, then God has foreknowledge. Confronted with this truth, open theists have three alternatives: (1) they can reject the passage's inspiration, (2) they can say that Jeremiah was using hyperbole to legitimize his prophetic role, or (3) they can claim that God was simply claiming *a posteriori* knowledge. Neither one of these alternatives speaks well of open theists' reliability on the inerrancy of Scripture. If Jeremiah's statement is truthful, then God has foreknowledge, and there are not enough theological gymnastics that can deny this biblical doctrine.

Jeremiah's calling was not an accident of nature. God foreknew the prophet's character qualities, gifts, and faith before he was born. Either God's revelation is truthful, or it's not: "Let God be true and every man a liar" (Rom. 3:4). Either God knew Jeremiah before he was conceived, or he did not. If God did not know the prophet before his birth, then God exaggerated or lied. God must have known the type of man the prophet would become to have appointed him as a prophet to the nations, or his revelation is not reliable. Jeremiah's example affirms that God's foreknowledge is more specific, and clear than the open view is willing to accept.

We can have a similar discussion regarding Paul's calling. The Bible states that God knew these men before they were born. Boyd suggests that God's calling of Jeremiah and Paul was conditional. He suggests that their callings were exhaustively settled only if they chose to obey God.[151] I do not know if Boyd understands the consequences of this statement. He appears to suggest that God was able to settle Jeremiah and Paul's futures only after their obedience. Not only that, if God settled these men's futures after their obedience, how could God claim to have known and called them before their conception? This is not possible within open view theology.

The God of the possible does not know if people will disobey later in life and, therefore, cannot settle any person's end state. The God of openness cannot offer any guarantees. He simply does not know how people will respond beyond the present. That was Pinnock's point when he suggested that God did not know that Abraham truly believed God until the very moment that the patriarch lifted the knife to sacrifice Isaac (discussed earlier). That was an asinine statement. I agree that obedience is always a requirement with God's calling, but this is precisely the point of foreknowledge. God knew ahead of time that upon calling Jeremiah and Paul, they would respond in faith and follow with obedience.

God foreknew their faith, and he chose to make this fact known to us. In other words, God could choose to say the same thing about every new believer in Jesus. This, however, is not necessary because two examples are enough to prove the point. That is, God has always foreknown the people who would respond in faith when presented with the gospel. This is the reason, I believe, Paul used the following order in election in the book of Romans. He wrote,

> And we know that for those who love God all things work together for good, for those who are called according to his purpose. For those whom he foreknew he also predestined to be conformed to the image of his Son, in order that he might be the firstborn among many brothers. And those whom he predestined he also called, and those whom he called he also justified, and those whom he justified he also glorified. (Rom. 8:27–30)

Paul makes two initial statements that are expanded in verses 28–30. He first states that "for those who love God all things work together for good." Then, he adds that those who love God "are called according to

---

[151] Boyd, 38–39.

his purpose." God's purpose cannot be anything other than God's method of salvation by grace through faith in Christ. The entire predestination issue (if you prefer—the exhaustive settled-ness of the future) is predicated on foreknowledge.

Paul stated that "those whom he foreknew he also predestined to be conformed to the image of his Son." God's foreknowledge of those who would love him (v. 27) settled their future resurrection as predestined. But what did God foreknow? I believe God foreknew the elect, both as individuals and as people who would exercise faith. God foreknew that many would believe upon hearing the gospel, and based on his perfect knowledge, "He ... predestined [them] to be conformed to the image of his Son." There is only one way this passage is true about God's salvation plan—God foreknew those who would believe before he created Adam and Eve, and on that score, he sent Jesus for them. Jesus said, "And this is the will of him who sent me, that I should *lose* nothing of all that he has given me but raise it up on the last day" (Jn. 12:25, emphasis added). When did God give them to Jesus? I believe Jesus received them before the foundation of the world, and he will lose not one of them. Hallelujah!

Open theists take a different approach. They must believe that God's claim of prior knowledge in these two instances is not truthful or that God was just bragging about something he could not have possibly known. Either God had definite and exhaustive knowledge of these two men's characters, as well as the faith response of all believers for all times before they were born, or He dissembled.

In order to advance the position that Paul's calling was conditional, Boyd misrepresents Paul's words to King Agrippa by suggesting that "he [Paul] could have disobeyed God's calling."[152] Boyd claimed the apostle's words are an indication that Paul had the option to reject the calling. Since Paul had this open-ended option, God could not have been sure about Paul's response in faith. I disagree. God's knowledge is not in question in this passage, and open theists know it. This is a gross misrepresentation of Paul's words. The apostle's actual words were, "I was not disobedient to the vision from heaven" (Acts 26:19). While it can be argued that disobedience was an open option for

---

[152] Boyd, 39.

Paul, the apostle's emphasis is placed on his obedience to the calling, not on his option to disobey. The apostle's statement was to make a contrast between his obedience and Agrippa's disobedience who had rejected the gospel clearly presented to him.

Paul was not highlighting his ability to frustrate God. His emphasis was placed on his willingness to submit to God's purpose for his life, which is what God had foreknown about Paul. He was sharing his faith with Agrippa, not his potential for disobedience. Theoretically, Paul and Jeremiah could have disobeyed God, but then God's claim regarding their calling before their birth, and their subsequent obedience, would be a farce. Paul's testimony is given precisely to affirm God's foreknowledge. Any other interpretation does hermeneutical violence to the text. This is the bottom-line issue here: if either Jeremiah or Paul had disobeyed, no one would have cared about them. They would have just been two more anonymous men that rejected God's grace.

Boyd's explanation does not properly account for God's claim that he called these men before their births. Obviously, it is not possible for God to make a literal calling of anyone before their birth, if all we are talking about is the presentation of God's message. Clearly, neither Jeremiah nor Paul had heard the message before their births, and yet God states that he called them before their births. I believe God revealed what he had foreknown about Jeremiah and Paul. Their calling are two perfect examples of God's foreknowledge. God called them before their birth because knew ahead of time that they would become God's representatives for the nations.

Let's Play Along

Let us go along with Boyd's premise that Paul intended to leave open the door for disobedience. If Paul had rejected God's calling, we would not be speaking about his great choice to disobey God. He would have become a nonfactor in Christian history. Additionally, if Paul had chosen disobedience, nobody would have cared who he was. We know about Paul because of his faith, which is to this day the mark of those called according to God's purpose, which is to say, the calling of those who hear the message and respond to it. Paul and Jeremiah are examples of men who chose to obey God and whose obedience was foreknown by God.

Agrippa and the Egyptian Pharaoh, on the other hand, are examples of men who chose to disobey God. It is interesting to note that God also foreknew Pharaoh's disobedience and revealed as much to Moses. Read it with me.

> But I know that the king of Egypt will not let you go unless a mighty hand compels him. So, I will stretch out my hand and strike the Egyptians with all the wonders that I will perform among them. After that, he will let you go (Ex. 3:19–20).

Clearly, Moses's writing indicated that God revealed to him Pharaoh's disobedience while Moses was still in Midian. The God of the open view could not have revealed Pharaoh's disobedience to Moses. But the God that spoke to Moses from the burning bush foreknew Pharaoh's unbelief in the same way he foreknew Paul's and Jeremiah's faith (Ex. 3:19). As a practical matter, it appears that if God did not know the future, he could not have assured Moses of Pharaoh's hardening of heart.

The problem for open theism is that, regardless of whether Paul was free to obey or disobey, God foreknew his faith, and the Bible states as much. Regardless of whether—technically—Pharaoh could have believed or not, God foreknew his disobedience and predicted it to Moses. This is the bottom line: if Paul had chosen disobedience, God would have known of his choice beforehand, and we would not be having this conversation about Paul's so-called option to disobey. If Pharaoh had believed, God would have known of his belief beforehand, and he would have been called according to God's purpose. This is precisely the reason that God was able to make the predictions—he knew what each man would choose. Thus, Paul and Jeremiah were called according to God's purpose, but Pharaoh and Agrippa were not. And God foreknew the faith responses from all four.

A Definition of Faith

Let me share a brief definition of *faith* here. Faith is, in its most simple form, taking God at his word.[153] The gospel message is being preached all over the world, and all who hear it and receive it have the same opportunity for repentance. However, only those who respond in faith will be saved. These are the ones God foreknew would believe.

Experience has shown that some will repent of their sins and that others will reject salvation. Since God is always the initiator of salvation, he gave his Son as the vehicle for salvation. The preaching of the gospel is a non-negotiable command for the church, for "how are they to believe in him of whom they have never heard?" (Rom. 10:14). God expects people to make a decision by faith regarding Christ based on the fact that he gave men and women the necessary tools, gifts, and volition to make a free choice of faith. Since people were created with the capacity to accept or reject God, they are without excuse.

God, then, is justified in holding people accountable for their rejection of Christ. The classical view, in its most extreme expression, suggests that God is the direct cause of both repentance and rejection. This assertion would make God the direct causal agent for both salvation and condemnation. Regardless of its historical tradition, the previous statement cannot be true about an impartial God. The Bible describes people's unbelief as born from within the sinfulness, not stemming from God (Rom. 7:18–20). Therefore, since every person born has a measure of faith, there is no biblical support for a theology that claims that God is the primary causal agent for people's unbelief that leads to their condemnation. Unbelief, like belief, comes from the heart. Paul said it this way.

> But what does it say? "The word is near you, in your mouth and in your heart" (that is, the word of faith that we proclaim); because, if you confess with your mouth that Jesus is Lord and *believe in your heart* that God raised him from the dead, you will be saved. For *with the heart one believes* and is justified, and with the mouth one confesses and is saved. (Rom. 10:8–10 ESV)

---

[153] Victor R. Scott, 2005.

The Potter's Analogy

There also appears to be widespread misinterpretation of the potter's analogy in Romans 9. If God has mercy on whom he has mercy, then, Paul asks, "Why does God still blame us?" (Rom. 9:19). That is, if salvation is a product of God's having mercy on some, on what basis does God find fault against those who do not receive his mercy? Paul anticipated the question of those who would misunderstand the passage. Paul basically stated that God "blames us," or holds us responsible, because we have sinned and are guilty.

However, in order for human culpability to be based on impartial justice, a person must have the capacity to recognize the difference between right and wrong. And if people are able to recognize their sins (the wrong), they also must have an alternative to exercise the faith that will remedy their condition. Faith is like air and water—every person has access to this gift from God. I believe faith is a gift intrinsic to being human. That is, everyone has faith. We can exercise faith, but we cannot exercise saving grace on ourselves. God created us with the capacity to believe—this is God's gift of faith to us. Then, he extended his grace to us—that is the gift of salvation made manifest through Jesus's life, death, and resurrection.

Again, personalization is the most common mistake with the misinterpretations of the potter's analogy. I am not claiming an exclusive understanding of this analogy. However, I do believe the analogy deals with the general principle of humanity's creation and that it is not a reference to God's active and daily involvement in each person's life. God is the potter and we are the clay in that God created Adam from the dust. The potter's analogy's main point is to illustrate that humans have no standing to "talk back to God" in protest of how they were created. God designed man in eternity past and created him from a lump of clay, "and it was good."

In this context, people do not have the right to talk back to God regarding the creation design or God's chosen method of salvation. Paul asks, "Shall what is formed say to the one who formed it, 'Why did you make me *like this?*'" The phrase "like this" is a reference to how God designed people as an integral part of this system we call creation. When did God make people "like this"? The obvious answer is found in the beginning, when God made Adam and Eve "like this." God did not consult any person when he designed humanity. In the same manner that the clay does not have a say in the potter's chosen design, humans did not play a role in God's design for creation.

Similarly, God did not consult people regarding his chosen salvation method. As a matter of fact, God never asked anyone whether they wanted to be born, where their preferred location for their birth was, or to what family they would like to belong. Once the procreation machine was set in motion, we became the byproduct of our ancestors, even though God knew each one of before creation. He knew when, where, and how we would be born. He knew the blessings and the struggles we would experience, and he did not preselect a group to receive greater blessing than another. He simply let the process develop and call to eternal life anyone who believes.

Actually, most people become conscious of their own existence when they are about three years old. With what authority do people dare "talk back to God"? People do not have a choice regarding the potter's activity in forming them because God's design was done according to the counsel of his will. People's future opinions about God's methods did not enter his mind. He brought humanity into existence before sin had entered the world, and we were designed to live in a world without sin. However, since God foresaw sin, he created the system in such a way that we could survive the ravages of sin until the appointed time of redemption.

Creation was, from beginning to end, an act of God's goodness. He created us to be in fellowship with him. But once created, Adam was not free to choose his own design. Adam could only choose the nature of his relationship with God. Adam chose to rebel. Paul stated that God made provision for salvation. "That if you confess with your mouth, 'Jesus is Lord,' and believe in your heart that God raised him from the dead, you will be saved" (Rom. 10:9). Every other religion promotes a salvation-by-works philosophy, but the Bible tells us that it is not up to people to choose their salvation method. If someone would like to be saved based on works or if he is upset about God's salvation plan, he is talking back to God (Rom. 9:20). In Christianity, God chose the salvation method: by grace through faith.

The parallel passage in Jeremiah is also misinterpreted. Boyd suggests that God changes in response to faith. He stated, "that the Lord is able and willing to adjust his plans with people just as the potter revises his plans for a vessel once his original plan was spoiled."[154] This is a nice try, but there is absolutely no evidence that God has changed his original design of humanity's creation. If the original plan was spoiled, then Boyd has the burden of proof to present the evidence that confirms that today's human beings have a different design and purpose than when God first created man in the garden.

There is no evidence the potter has made a different kind of person, and there is no evidence that humanity messed up the original design to the point that God had to go back to the drawing board to redesign people. The potter's analogy, in my estimation, is not about the day-to-day transformation people experience as they grow and mature in faith. While this is a fair application, it is not the primary purpose of the passage. Rather, the potter's analogy is about God's plan to create humans in a particular way. Boyd's application is irrelevant because it does not address the issue at hand, which is that God does not know the future. This analogy says nothing on behalf of open theism. The potter's analogy is a reference to the original creation of Adam and Eve, and there is no reason to speak of God's "changing his mind" regarding his original design. God saw that his design for humanity was good.

Even when Noah's civilization was destroyed, God did not change his original plan for humanity. That is, God continued his salvation process with the design he had originally created. He did not re-create humans as a different creature. After Noah, people continued to reproduce as before, and death continued to be passed on to the rest of humanity as before. People today are not different in kind from what they were in the garden of Eden. In order for Boyd's contention that God's design was *spoiled* to be true, he has to show evidence that a person's design today is different than his or her design before the flood. A better interpretation for the metaphor finds God working in and through *damaged vessels* to accomplish his will. The potter's design and work regarding humans is found in Genesis, and it continues to this day.

---

[154] Boyd, 141.

Then God said, "Let us make man in our image, in our likeness, and let them rule over the fish of the sea and the birds of the air, over the livestock, over all the earth, and over all the creatures that move along the ground." So, God created man in his own image, in the image of God he created him; male and female he created them. (Gen. 1:26–27)

The potter's work was finished on the sixth day of creation, "and it was very good" (Gen. 1:31). It was on the sixth day that the potter created the doll from the dust. That is what potters do—they work with clay. God's work with clay was completed on the sixth day of creation. After the potter (God) created man (the clay), he breathed on Adam, who became a living soul.

There is absolutely no support for the notion of God's changing his mind in the analogy of the potter and the clay because there is no evidence that God has redesigned people. Neither Jeremiah nor Paul were advancing a new revelation that God had changed his design of humanity's original creation. They were simply stating that humans are in no position to complain to God regarding how he chose to design and create them or how God chose to save them. This is not only a sensible interpretation of the analogy; it is the only one, in my estimation, that explains Paul's and Jeremiah's words within their context.

A challenge to the "deterministic interpretation" of Romans 9 is a necessary exercise. I hold that any deterministic interpretation of Romans 9 goes beyond the purpose of the text by personalizing Paul's words to apply to individuals. Boyd's interpretation that the potter (God) was *changing his mind* regarding humanity's creation does violence to the text. This is forced hermeneutics. Not one single passage of Scripture supports the idea that God recreated people into a different form.

In my opinion it is an error to interpret Jeremiah 18:5–10 to mean that God can change his mind regarding his promises, whether negative or positive. Let me quote the passage here.

Then the word of the LORD came to me: "O house of Israel, can I not do with you as this potter does?" declares the LORD. "Like clay in the hand of the potter, so are you in my hand, O house of Israel. *If* at any time I announce that a nation or kingdom is to be uprooted, torn down and destroyed, and if that nation I warned repents of its evil, then I will relent and not inflict on it the disaster I had planned. *And if* at another time I announce that a nation or kingdom is to be built up and planted, and if it does evil in my sight and does not obey me, then I will reconsider the good I had intended to do for it." (Jer. 18:5–10, emphasis added)

A closer look at the passage suggests that Jeremiah uses a conditional clause, which is a common method in some prophecies. The passage is not about God changing his mind but about his responding to human faith. God deals with us in the present, and while he will withhold a present blessing based on a present disobedience, God does not deny us a present blessing based on a future disobedience. If a person does not repent, then God is not obligated to send his blessing. But if the person repents, God receives him as a son. The passage in Jeremiah is not about God changing his mind. It is about God's commitment to honor faith and not to honor the faithless.

The passage describes God's faithfulness in his consistent response to people even when they are ambivalent in their faith to God. Thus, God remains faithful even when we are unfaithful (2 Tim. 2:13). Anybody can interpret passages in any way they want, but the interpretation by the open view of Jeremiah 18 is neither required, nor necessary, to properly understand the text. Additionally, this passage does not support openness theology's basic premise that God cannot know the future.

Conclusion

Open theists make a valiant attempt to present the open view as a mainstream theological position. I am not sure what their motives are, but I believe their efforts do not have the force they would like. Sadly, many Christians will be persuaded to follow this position without considering all the possible ramifications. Open view proponents may not intend to deceive people. However, they do want to convince a few to accept this position. They appear to have two basic goals: to give credibility to the open view as a legitimate and mainstream theological area of study, and to gain a few converts. In my estimation, open view theologians do not present a congruent hermeneutical case that could establish open theism as a sustainable theological system. However, since they are appealing to an emotional response to theology, I am sure many will consider joining their ranks. There are several reasons the open view should not stand as a theological system.

First, it cannot prove that God's foreknowledge is causative. There is no theological necessity to conclude that foreknowledge imposes an external compulsion in people's decision-making processes.

Second, the open view fails to make the case that it provides a better explanation for evil. If the God of foreknowledge is guilty for allowing any evil he could have prevented, the God of open theism is also guilty, because even though he has exhaustive knowledge of all possibilities, he chose not to stop the evil he must have known was inevitable.

Third, open theism does not add any new insight to the discussion about human freewill. Human freedom is not contingent upon God's foreknowledge because God is not the causal agent for human behavior. God exists outside the created system. Thus, the creatures trapped in this physical world cannot influence God.

Fourth, open theism discourages prayer. It describes God as unreliable in answering prayers since he does not control future unintended consequences. In Suzanne's case, the God of the open view answered her prayer without knowing her husband's character. This is truly inconceivable.

Fifth, the open view is not able to provide a coherent case that explains its own inherent contradictions. On the one hand, it asserts that the future does not exist and cannot be known. On the other hand, it affirms with the same conviction that God can "partly settle the future" and that God showed "remarkable knowledge" about Jesus's life in particular. This contradiction, regardless of how much it is tried, cannot be reconciled. The obvious problem for the open view is to explain how God is able to purpose to predetermine a future that includes human events that do not exist and cannot be known.

Finally, open theism as a theological system destroys the very gift of God we need the most—God's trustworthiness in times of trouble. If God's promises cannot be trusted, then there is no point in serving him. However, we hold that God knows the future and all the contingencies associated with it. This knowledge is of great comfort to God's children.

In addition to the above-stated reasons to reject open theism, we can cite the four major areas that open theists do not address in their defense of their system but that they must if they want to be taken more seriously. Allow me to reintroduce the four unresolved areas of open theism as we presented them in our introduction.

First, open theists must provide a clear definition of prophecy within their system. We are looking for precise definitions of terms and of how the God of the open view can predict anything that is related to people if he cannot know anything in the future related to humanity. Without prophecy, we cannot know how God's plan will unfold within human affairs because the God of open theism is ascertaining that very thing as we speak.

Second, open theists must answer how the God of open theism answers prayers that have unintended consequences, not only to the recipients of the answered prayers but also to God himself. Again, we need precise definitions of terms that go beyond the platitudes that open theism is more practical because God can answer prayers without knowing the ultimate consequences that those answers would have on the people who receive them.

Third, open theists have to explain how God's perfect knowledge of the present does not infringe on humanity's libertarian freewill in the present. They argue that if God has foreknowledge, by necessity, that knowledge will eliminate human freewill. If the principle is true about the future, it must also be true about the present.

Finally, open theists must also define how information possessed by *one* free agent becomes causative for the behavior of *another* free agent. In other words, they need to explain how information I might have could force someone else to act according to my information. This is simply experientially false about human interactions, and it is probably false regarding God's knowledge. They must be able to present a credible argument that demonstrates a direct cause-and-effect correlation between information and causality.

Each one of these categories destroys the basic premises of open theism. When we put them together, open theism is exposed for what it is—nothing more than a postmodern rehashing of Lorenzo McCabe's discredited nescient doctrine. After examining these four categories in open theism, we have concluded that open theism fails to provide a coherent argument that can refute God's knowledge, or affirm Jowers's present knowledge, much less find any support for McCabe's nescient principle.

God has frustrated scholars and laymen alike. When we think we have defined him, something new about his character emerges. Open theists' attempt to resolve their frustration with God has not had the desired results. They accomplished two unintended consequences for themselves: they have remained frustrated, and they have placed themselves outside the knowledge of the God of the Bible. It is true that we do not know everything we would like to know about God. But it is also true that we know enough of God to establish an eternal relationship with him. By all means, let us continue searching for the secrets of God, but let us not distort his character to the point that the God of the Bible becomes unrecognizable. I will conclude with Paul's frustration and hope. Paul wanted to know more, but he could not. However, he had hope that one day he would understand much more—when we will see Jesus "face to face."

> Love never ends. As for prophecies, they will pass away; as for tongues, they will cease; as for knowledge, it will pass away. For we know in part and we prophesy in part, but when the perfect comes, the partial will pass away. When I was a child, I spoke like a child, I thought like a child, I reasoned like a child. When I became a man, I gave up childish ways. For now, we see in a mirror dimly, but then face to face. Now I know in part; then I shall know fully, even as I have been fully known. So now faith, hope, and love abide, these three; but the greatest of these is love. (1 Cor. 13:8–13)

Author's Biography

Pastor Luis Scott graduated from Moody Bible Institute in 1986 with a Bachelor of Arts degree in Bible Theology with a Greek Emphasis. He received a Master of Divinity from Northern Baptist Theological Seminary in Lombard, Illinois, in June 1990. While serving the US army as a chaplain, Pastor Scott completed the Clinical Pastoral Education program at Eisenhower Medical Center. After twenty years of service, Pastor Scott retired from the army in July 2007. He is currently serving as Pastor and Founder of Ambassadors and Embajadores churches in Columbus, GA.